Married Lovers, Married Friends

Steve & Annie Chapman

With Maureen Rank

BETHANY HOUSE PUBLISHERS

MINNEAPOLIS, MINNESOTA 55438

Published by Bethany House Publishers
A Ministry of Bethany Fellowship International
11400 Hampshire Avenue South
Minneapolis, Minnesota 55438
www.bethanyhouse.com

Printed in the United States of America by
Bethany Press International, Minneapolis, Minnesota 55438

Library of Congress Cataloging-in-Publication Data

Chapman, Steve.
    Married lovers married friends / Steve and Annie Chapman, with
Maureen Rank.
        p.   cm.

    1. Marriage—Religious aspects—Christianity.
I. Chapman, Annie. II. Rank, Maureen. III. Title.
BV835.C46   1989
248.8′44—dc20   89–32729
ISBN 1–55661–047–5   CIP
ISBN 0–7642–2226–0 (pbk.)

We want to dedicate this book to the two couples
who have modeled love, committment, and caring—

Paul J. and Lillian M. Chapman
and
N. R. and Sylvia Williamson,

married nearly 90 years combined,
have taught us that we can be married
and still remain friends.
Mom, Dad, we publically honor you
and call you blessed.

To our children,

Nathan and Heidi,

we offer our sincere love and appreciation.
You two are the best traveling buddies
and you make our lives together
a triumphant demonstration
of what love is all about.

STEVE AND ANNIE CHAPMAN were married in 1975 and became a part of the popular singing group "Dogwood." In 1981 their music took a new direction and they began to minister as a couple to families. They have several albums distributed nationally, their music and message on the family has been featured in numerous magazines, and they perform at a pace of over 100 concerts across the nation each year. They make their home in Nashville with their two children.

MAUREEN RANK is a graduate of Iowa State University and spent six years on the Navigators' staff ministering to college students. She is author of six books, including *God Can Make It Happen* and *Free to Grieve*. She and her husband live in Knoxville, Iowa, and have two children.

Contents

A Remotely Good Marriage

ANNIE: When the evening started, neither Steve nor I expected we'd end it glaring at each other. And embarrassingly enough, the issue we feuded over wasn't something as major as money, or mothers-in-law, or the way to world peace. We wound up filling the room with emotional icicles over—well, you won't believe it.

The evening began innocently enough. Our family was eagerly tuning-in the Summer Olympics—at least Steve and our children were. I'm not much of a sports enthusiast, but I knew it was my duty as a loyal patriot to watch the games, so I joined Steve and the kids in the family room. I sat down beside my beloved and began to force an interest in the games.

A few minutes passed and I found my loyalty drifting. But then I saw it—there it was on the table, the scepter of authority powered by two AA batteries, the remote control. I knew it would salvage my evening. With power in hand, I waited for a commercial and then began my search for other entertainment. As I flipped through the channels

I happened onto an old movie I'd wanted to see for awhile. Two channels later, I found a documentary highlighting some pressing, national issue I thought I ought to be informed about. Just before I got to the platform diving competition I bypassed one of our family's favorite sitcoms.

We'd barely started watching the sitcom when a commercial interrupted. Not wanting to waste time hearing a sales pitch for a car I did not need, I touched a button and switched over to the documentary to catch a moment or two. As soon as the documentary went to commercial, I flipped back to the Olympics.

But the network was covering equestrian competition, which didn't interest me. I knew the documentary would still be in the midst of commercials, so I once again punched the remote and found the sitcom.

Well, it only took a minute or two for me to realize I'd seen this episode before, so I zapped the channel over to see how the movie was progressing.

"Annie, we were watching the Olympics," Steve complained.

"Yeah, I know," I nodded, my eyes glued to the set. "We'll get back to it in a minute. I just need to see how this movie starts so I'll know what's happening if the Olympics don't get more interesting." I watched for a minute or two. Satisfied, I flipped to the documentary. (These are moments when an uncanny sense of just how long a commercial will last comes in handy!) We caught what, to me, was a key list of statistics, so when they started droning on about "sociological implications," I cut away to the sitcom.

"Annie . . ." Steve's voice had taken on a harder edge. "The Olympics . . .!"

"They've finished all the good stuff," I explained to him as patiently as I could, which wasn't easy while I was trying to remember what happened next in the sitcom so

I could decide whether or not this would be a good time to check in again on the Olympics.

That was it.

Steve went for the remote control in my hand. But he neither understood that I have the mental capability of watching five shows at the same time while keeping them all straight in my head, nor did he realize how quickly I can move when someone goes for the remote.

Steve and I lead seminars on marriage, so in the interest of preserving a portion of our credibility, I'll spare you a jab-by-jab account of the argument that followed. You'll probably get the picture if I tell you that later that night, when the news ironically reported about a man killing his girlfriend in a tussle over their remote control, Steve had a most sadistic gleam in his eye. (He was probably remembering what Mrs. Billy Graham had said when she was asked whether she'd ever considered divorce. "No," she replied, "but I've thought of murder!")

Later, when we were speaking again, we both realized how silly and thoughtless we'd been toward each other.

This is typical of married couples everywhere. Like you, we shouted our "I do's" from hearts bursting with love and hopes high as the mid-July temperatures of our wedding day. But add a few years, house payments, fifteen extra pounds, two kids, and too much to do and—well. Let's say we've seen things firsthand—two people who started out in love can wind up bitter enemies unless you take action to keep love and friendship growing.

A minister was asked to officiate at the funeral of a woman he'd never met. When he arrived at the funeral parlor, the dead woman's husband stood alone by her casket. The minister knew nothing about the couple except that they had been married fifty-seven years. So for lack of a better word of comfort, he approached the husband and said, "Fifty-seven years is a long time."

"Too long," the old widower replied flatly. "She was meaner than blazes."[1]

We laugh because we all know at least one marriage like this. But God never intended marriage to wear the shine off a love affair. He designed marital oneness as a haven where love can blossom into its full beauty. He intended that husbands and wives be lovers and friends for all their lives.

In the pages ahead, we want you to join us in our journey toward making marriage all that God intended. As we share our struggles, we hope you'll feel less alone in your daily battles. We hope, too, that as you see some directives the Lord has given us for growing together, you'll come away with increased faith.

Love does not have to die. Like us, you too can discover that your marriage can be continually remade with God's ever-present help.

In fact, it may be that your marriage is about to be born anew and the two of you will rediscover an excitement in your relationship which was designed by God himself and meant to be known only in the context of marriage.

Married Lovers

Her heart was poundin'; he called her on the
    phone.
They made their secret plans to spend the night
    alone.
She fills his passions,
He fills her dreams,
I know what you may be thinkin'—
But it's not what it seems,
'Cause they're . . .

---

[1]Gordon MacDonald, *Happiness Is Growing a Marriage* (Kansas City: Beacon Hill Press), 77.

Married Lovers—
They have a right to this romance.
Married lovers—
Don't have to worry when they dance.
Married lovers—
There's no sin in what they do,
'Cause heaven gives its blessings to this holy
    rendezvous.

Nobody's bein' cheated, nobody cries,
And when they see each other,
Won't be nobody tellin' lies.
She fills his passions,
He fills her dreams,
Their love is pure as silver inside the
    "golden ring."[2]

[2]"Married Lovers," Lyrics by Steve Chapman. Used by permission.

You Can't Be Married on the Backstroke

STEVE: During my daze in skool, spelling wuz never my best coarse.

But when someone asks me to spell "love"—that one I'm sure to get right. Real love has to consist of T–I–M–E.

You can't build a relationship with anyone unless you continue to spend *time* together. We know that instinctively when we're dating, but when we marry we assume time together is no longer necessary.

Nothing could be further from the truth! But this was a lesson I had to learn the hard way.

When Annie and I got married, I was a traveling musician. This proved to be no detriment to our bliss because I'd had the good sense to choose a woman who could sing like an angel, understood my ministry and wanted to make it hers as well. Annie just threw her suitcase in the van, and off we went. We didn't have to make any major choices, so we could give each other time. We could roll on with life, each doing what we did best, and still find ourselves together nearly twenty-four hours a day. And we'd both had enough relational experience to know how to use the time we had to build bonds between us. (We'll talk more about that later . . . what to *do* with the time to make it worth something.)

But back to the Chapmans, happily chugging down the highway of life. After all this time together, not surprisingly, Annie became pregnant, so we knew some changes were in the offing. Nathan's arrival forced us to think over what kind of life God wanted for our family.

One thing we believed. God didn't intend our children to be an afterthought, crammed here and there into the leftover crannies of our schedules. We'd known people who'd left their children behind when they took to the road, using rationale like "the importance of God's work," and "quality time is what matters, not quantity time." But both Annie and I knew God didn't give us a child so someone else could raise him. And we also believed ministering to *our* family was every bit as important to God as our ministry to *other* families.

So we decided together that I'd go on with the group, and Annie would stay with Nathan. Though Annie and I knew we'd miss each other terribly, she'd come to see parenting as a calling of God every bit as important as the public ministry we were doing, or maybe more important. She didn't believe she could do a good job mothering and traveling as well, so settling at home seemed like the only way we could do it all.

When Annie left the group, it took no less than a five-piece band to replace her. Now, with seven families to support, the group had to be on the road fifteen to twenty days a month just to meet expenses. So I found myself gone from my wife and child seventy-five percent of the time.

I did what I could to stay close to them, though. I'd call home every day and worked hard at sending cards and letters while I was gone so they'd know how much I was thinking of them. And when I was home, I'd try to compensate by making our time together special.

Annie worked hard to make a go of it, too. Because she didn't want to stand in the way of my work and ministry, she'd cheerily push me out the door on the days I'd have to go.

What she didn't tell me was that as soon as the door would close behind me, she'd head for the bathroom and throw up. She didn't tell me, either, that while I traveled, her periods stopped. And she didn't let me know about the many nights she cried herself to sleep from loneliness.

Our son also started showing the effects of his daddy's absence. We made jokes about Nathan learning his numbers by counting the days till his dad came home. But to a little child, it was no joke. He was learning that his dad wasn't a real parent to be counted on. Once when I reprimanded him, he shot back, "Old man, why don't you just get back in that motor home and go on another trip?" Corrections that meant something came from Mom, not this shadowy figure who appeared now and again from the door of a motor home or in the photo on an album cover.

If there ever was a moment in our lives when we looked like the typical American couple, this was it. Husband giving his best energy to earning a living; wife giving her best energy to raising the kids; home little more than a refueling station and message center. (We knew a couple who never fought . . . because they were *never* together! And we weren't far from being just like them.) We chose to live like this from wonderful Christian motives, but the toll it took on our marriage was no less than if we'd been unbelievers.

And I felt miserable. But how could I do the ministry I felt I'd been given, and still give time to my family? I pleaded with God for a better answer than the one we'd tried. And little by little I began to see I had a decision to make. Would my family have to accommodate my work, or was work going to accommodate my family? When I understood that God intended my family be first, I knew I'd have to leave the group. So, thirty minutes before a concert in Decatur, Illinois, I told the guys in the band I was giving my six-month notice.

From a human standpoint, making this decision was one of the scariest things I've ever done. In one fell swoop, I'd cut myself off from my source of employment, my income, and my career, but all for the sake of my family. As we drove back to Nashville that night, I had about as much tranquillity as a man facing a firing squad. Was I doing the right thing?

We arrived home early Sunday morning, and since Annie had already left for Sunday school, I asked the guys to drop me off at our church. I dragged into the building, loaded down with all the fears and questions that only a man who has just quit his job and has no prospects for the future can understand. Fortunately, our Sunday school class was watching a film and the room was dark, so at least I knew Annie wouldn't be able to see the worry on my face when I walked in.

But just as I stepped into our classroom, and slid into a seat beside my wife, the man on the screen looked straight at me (or at least that's how it seemed) and said pointedly, "How can you be a good husband and father if you're never home?" Honest—those were his exact words!

At that second, I knew how the disciples must have felt at the Resurrection. I *was* doing the right thing! My decision might mean I'd have to trade my guitar for a lifetime of selling shoes, but that sacrifice would be small compared to the fulfillment of knowing I was finally making my wife and child the high priority the Lord wanted them to be.

You've guessed what happened next, right? On the scene bursts a big producer from the Hot-Selling Gospel Record Company who offers Annie and me a big-bucks contract and our own Nashville recording studio, complete with back-up singers and an adjoining nursery.

That's not exactly how it went. I took a low-paying slot in a jingle company writing advertising ditties, and we scratched along on $750 a month. But Annie and I made up for lost time, learning how to give our relationship the attention the Lord intended it to have.

I was still able to do some singing on the side, though. And as I did, the desire began to fester in me to have Annie singing, too. I knew the kind of musical gift she'd been given, and I began to feel increasingly frustrated that it wasn't being used.

Annie, however, wasn't the least bit frustrated. She'd been called to be a mom—so a *mom*, and no more, was what she was going to be. Because by now little Heidi had come into our lives. But she agreed to try singing together in order to please me.

Everything we did, the Lord seemed to smile on. God began to stir in her, prodding her toward the possibility that even though He wanted us together, it might not be in our little house in Nashville. She began to wonder if maybe He was saying we should take to the road—and take the kids with us.

Saying yes to this idea was every bit as scary for Annie as leaving the group had been for me. But because of her commitment to the Lord and to the priority of our marriage, she finally agreed. So we packed up the young'uns in a little blue van, and off we went. The rest, as they say, is history.

Of course, in most history books, you hear more about

the triumphs than you do the tragedies. In our case, living with a preschooler and a baby crammed into the back of a van leaned far more heavily to the side of tragedy—or hilarity, depending on how you looked at it. Like the time I nearly ruined our welcome because of a bout with the potty chair.

If you've been through the toilet-training phase of child-rearing, you know this is one arena where the trainee calls all the shots (literally). When he's gotta go, he's gotta go. So to accommodate nature's beckoning, we plunked a potty chair in the middle of the van. It would serve its purpose; then to make the trip bearable, we'd empty the thing as soon as we'd stop.

Which brought us to the time we'd pulled up to a church where we were to perform, and I was assigned potty chair clean-up duty. So I picked the thing up and headed for the church to find a restroom. All would have gone well, except I forgot I was not dealing here with our old familiar chair. (We'd left the other one sitting on top of the trailer on our last trip. When we drove off, it slid off and smashed on the cement. We'd made a K-Mart stop to acquire some new equipment. But I'd failed to notice this new chair had no safety bar on the back to hold the bowl in place like our old one had.) So I wrangled open the heavy church door, and just as I stepped inside, the bowl slid out of the back of the potty chair, dumping all its unsavory contents right toward the brand-new plush carpet. It looked as though I'd deliberately opened the door and emptied the potty out on the floor.

If I'd never believed in God before, that moment would have been enough to convince me He was alive, because all that foul stuff "just happened" to land right in the middle of a large plastic mat positioned inside the door. An innocent-looking teenaged boy also "just happened" to be sweeping the stairs nearby. I screamed at him, "Grab that end of the mat!" He gingerly picked up one end while I took the other, and we navigated our sloshy, smelly cargo to the restroom.

Unbelievably, not a drop of it spilled. We later found out the pastor was so protective of their new carpet, he wouldn't even let people drink coffee in that part of the church, lest they soil the rug. Imagine the warm feelings he'd experience toward the traveling musicians if he discovered they'd nearly splashed his precious carpet with. . . . Oh, my.

But these inconveniences—and we could tell you about hundreds—were a small price to pay for the privilege of having our family together.

When Annie and I did our first album, one critic said, "The Chapmans sound like two soloists that just happen to be singing the same song at the same time." He was pointing out that our blend wasn't as easy as it should have been and, unhappily, he was right. We *are* two voices that sound best alone. If our music came first in our lives, we might not work together professionally. But we've had to go back to our belief that God intends that our work adapt to our family, not the other way around. So we've *learned* to sing together, and just like the other parts of our married life, practice has helped us find better ways to blend.

Anything nice has its price. Part of the price we all have to pay to put our marriage and family first is to be out-of-sync with the rest of Western civilization. And, in the short-term, there may not be many obvious rewards. If you've struggled trying to get your priorities in order, you'll take comfort in the fact that many others have faced the same dilemma.

Giving up other things to be at home sometimes doesn't pay off as we expected. We received this letter from a father who decided to take a stab at making his family more important:

> During [your] concert I determined to spend the next day, Saturday, my day off, playing with my children (ages 6, 3, and 1½) all day. I was up coloring and building block houses much earlier than I expected. At 10:00 A.M. we were still going strong. My 18-month-old son was about to knock down my six-year-old son's castle. So I scooped up my 18-month-old son and instead of shutting him out of the fun behind a gate, I remembered your concert and playfully swooped him up onto my head and twirled him around the room.
>
> It was at that moment my wife walked in and informed me that my 18-month-old son, who was sitting on my head, had a load in his pants that was soaking into my hair. My nose said she wasn't lying. I passed him to my wife, sprinted for the bathroom, jumped in the shower, turned on the water . . . and found only cold water due to my wife doing loads of laundry that morning. As I stood there freezing, I wondered if this was the "family fun" you had spoken about the night before. . . .

The pressure is on us to have it all, do it all, and be it all. And though I feel this pressure as a man, Annie reminds me of how exceptionally difficult it is right now for women to stand against this tide of rising expectations that take us away from each other.

She insists that if you compiled a profile of the Woman of the Eighties from television, magazines and talk shows, she'd look like this: She'd be a beautiful, alluring woman who constantly fulfills all her husband's fantasies, as well as her own. She's also a wonderfully devoted mother who finds her "quality time" with her children always in great quantity. Her children never have dirt on their faces, never eat peanut butter sandwiches for lunch, never get served the heel of the bread, don't wear hand-me-down clothes, make straight A's and play the cello. Her home, of course, looks like the centerfold of *Southern Living* magazine.

For *this* woman there's no ordinary job outside the home. She's lunging up the corporate ladder in an exciting career. Her job may demand seventy hours a week, but she always comes home looking fresh and beautiful.

In her off hours, she serves as councilwoman for her district and president of the PTA. She bakes cookies for all the school functions, volunteers for the class field trips, sings in the church choir and teaches Sunday school. Of course she fits in workouts at the spa five days a week, so she looks like a walking Diet Coke commercial. And while she's shrinking her waistline, she is also expanding her mind, taking law courses at the university.

Isn't it too bad that we Christians buy into this neurotic frenzy by pulling out Proverbs 31 and using it to beat women into a quaking mass of guilt, insisting it's *spiritual* to have such impossible standards of achievement? We use the woman Solomon describes in Proverbs 31 to turn Superwoman into a saint.

Annie tells me she used to hate this Proverbs 31 woman because the dear lady seems to have it all together. She's beautiful, strong, well-organized, maternal, matrimonial and managerial at the same time. Annie said once, "She put a load on me I just couldn't carry."

But Annie has made her peace with this capable woman. The breakthrough came the day she realized that the woman's children "rise up and call her blessed." Annie decided right then this woman must be older, and probably post-menopausal. Annie said, "My kids don't rise and call me blessed. They rise up and call me to fix them some breakfast! But when my children are grown, *then* they'll call me 'blessed,' just as I now do my own mother. Then I'll probably have energy to take on some challenges I can't during these years of child-rearing."

Both Christian men and women have tough choices to make about the priority of their marriage. In light of the obstacles confronting us, we use two simple ideas to help us keep our life together at the top of our list.

First, we try to cut out junk activities. You've heard of junk food? Well, junk activities are the ones that don't fit with what we have to have for a healthy marriage. What are you doing that might not really have to be done? Is it *urgent* that the house be spotless seven days a week? Do both cars *have* to be washed and waxed every Saturday? Sure they're important—but important enough to rob your family of good times together?

Even worthy activities can become junk if they duplicate other things we're already doing. After all, you can get sick on eating too much of perfectly nutritious foods! So, what are you doing that others could do if you didn't? Is there no one else at all who can sit in on all those church committee meetings if you withdrew? Will the world be worse off if you quit volunteering for those civic organizations?

Second, we try to keep down junk expenditures. One of the greatest pressures that invades our family life comes in the push to have a paycheck that covers the life we *want* to lead. There are two ways to increase your income: work more, or spend less. We try hard to keep our expenses down, for the sake of our time together.

If the Lord has enabled you to provide an abundance of things without taking away from the priority of your marriage, I'm not trying to make you feel guilty. But as a report in *Fortune* magazine puts it, "Couples complain that they have everything except time together." And this is the same complaint we hear from men and women all across America. Your family needs your *presence* much more than they need your *presents*. And your spouse needs more from you than just someone to help with the kids. He or she needs you to be companion and friend and lover, in the way you were before the kids came along.

Make your life together a priority, so you won't look at each other when the kids are gone, and ask, "Who are you?"

Their hearts were broken as they told her goodbye,
Then they stood in the yard 'til she drove out of
     sight.
Then they turned to face their first day and night
Of their last child leavin' home.

She made some coffee and he went outside,
And all afternoon they never met eyes.
And it was late in the evenin' when she realized
They hadn't spoken all day.

Then she looked at the photograph over their bed
Of the children she could say she knew.
Then, she looked at the stranger asleep in her bed
And whispered, "Who are you?"

Years ago all they had was each other.
They were best of friends and the best of lovers.
Then their good times made them father and
     mother,
And they did the job so well.

But lost in the details of raisin' the kids
Was the thing of most value that lovers can give:
Keepin' each other's needs at the top of the list
Of the things they've gotta do.

He was the first to wake up the next mornin'
In a house as quiet as a tomb.
Then, he looked at the stranger asleep in his bed,
And whispered, "Who are you?"

But it's not too late for fathers and mothers
To go back to bein' best friends and lovers.
It's sad when they whisper, "Who are you?"

Put each other's needs at the top of the list.
Do those lovin' things so easy to miss
And don't forget to whisper, "I love you."[1]

Romance Starts With a Servant's Heart

STEVE: Ah, romance! I remember the passionate sighs, the $400 long-distance telephone bills and roses for no reason. The feeling that life began the day *she* walked into my dreary existence.

How I remember when those emotions first began to churn in me for Annie, the woman who would become my wife. I sent her flowers, told her she was beautiful, and even came to a complete stop at all the stop signs when she rode with me. Romance was bustin' out all over, and it was grand. I determined to do whatever it took to make this woman mine.

"What I did for love" (Chapman-style).

This woman of my dreams was born a country girl. And not just one of those why-don't-you-stand-next-to-the-tractor-for-the-camera-honey kind of country girls you see on television, either. Annie grew up on a dairy farm so rural it could make "Walton's Mountain" look like downtown Cincinnati. In comparison, I was nearly a city slicker—from Chapmanville, West Virginia (population 3,000).

But I was determined to do whatever it took to impress this beautiful girl's farmer-father. It didn't take many weekend visits to their farm to figure out that keeping the cows milked took up most of everyone's concentration night and day, 365 days a year. That was it! I'd get out to the barn and help with the milking, and Annie's dad would love me forever. So off I trudged one morning—at 4:30!

Now Annie had been at this farm stuff a lot longer than I had. There was my delicate beloved—slipping between those pungent, 1500-pound cows with a ten-penny nail in her hand, poking and pushing them around with the skill of a seasoned cowpuncher in the middle of the roundup. How she managed, while still avoiding those piles of stuff the cows had so carelessly deposited on the floor, was beyond me. I looked down at my new white tennis shoes and concluded I'd better find some other way to help.

Then I found it! Over in the corner sat a steaming bucket of water with a rag in it. Once before, I'd seen Annie's dad using the rag to wipe off the cows' udders. I assumed he was washing off the "spigots" before he hooked the milking machine onto them. What I didn't know was that on a cold West Virginia morning in March those bovine milk faucets needed help letting go of the milk. A little massage with a warm rag stimulated the flow.

But it looked like they were in need of a good cleaning to me. At last!—a job I could do without the danger of stepping in cow-doo. So I grabbed the bucket and headed for the milk-house sink for a refill of clean water.

I never expected to be nominated for secretary of agriculture, but I did know a thing or two about cleaning. I knew, for instance, that if warm water cleans well, hot water cleans twice as good. So I turned on the faucet and let the water run over one hand until it was too hot to touch, then filled the bucket. I figured that cows have thick hides, so the hotter the better. With a smug grin, I plunked the steaming bucket down next to Ol' Number 32. (All the cows had earrings with their numbers on them so you could tell which one was which.) I gave 32 a nudge and said, "You're next, sweetheart."

When I pulled the rag from the bucket, it was so hot I could hardly hold it. But what did a little pain matter? If a little suffering would win my future father-in-law, then suffer I would. So I wrung out that blistering rag and slapped it underneath, on Ol' 32's tender parts.

Then the lights went out.

When I came to, Annie's dad told me how impressed he was with my effort—but I didn't ever need to come back at milking time again! Her family still affectionately refers to it as "the time Steve tried to sterilize the dairy herd."

I'll bet you have a story or two of your own about some "udderly" ridiculous thing romance drove you to do. If only this delicious state of emotional insanity was as easy to maintain as it is to fall into.

Secrets Hallmark never told you.

An engaged couple strolls down the street, hand in hand, pretty as a greeting card. Accidentally, the little lady steps on her man's foot. As he pulls her spike heel out of his arch, he gushes, "Don't worry about it, sweetheart. I've got a second foot right over here. Think nothing of it." Is he offended? Never! He seizes the opportunity to show her how incredibly tough he is in the face of pain.

Now let's fast-forward to their fifth wedding anniversary. They're walking down this same street, and she's wearing those same shoes. Yike! She plants that spike right back into the hole in his foot she bored before. But this time as he pulls the heel out, he gives her a look that would smack King Kong into submission. "Just because you look like Bigfoot don't mean you have to walk like him, too!" he snarls. "Why don'cha watch where you're goin'?"

And he isn't the only one who's lost the romance. When she heard him say, "Wilt thou. . . ?", she wilted. The problem is, she hasn't revived since.

Unfortunately, romance seems to be a premarital condition that is cured instantly by a trip to the altar. A woman in one of our marriage seminars once gave this definition of romance: "It's the attraction during courtship that vanishes with the words 'I do.' " Most couples take "I do" to mean "Maybe I *did* when I was still trying to woo you, but I sure *don't* intend to anymore!"

Those of us who believe in Christ often don't do much better, sad to say. As I've heard a popular Christian speaker say:

> To dwell above with saints we love
> Now, won't that be glory?
> But to live below with those we know . . .
> Well, that's another story!

Where does the romance go?

What happened? Why did the romance fade?

We believe it's because we've been injected with a massive overdose of soap opera syrup, and it's brainwashed us into believing romance comes from a Fourth of July fireworks of feelings, blasted into the sky by a megacharge of hormones and heavy breathing. We sigh over those fuzzy pictures Hallmark produces of boy and girl romping through a meadow awash with daisies, and conclude we know the elements necessary to generate romance.

The marrieds we meet often voice these "the moon shone in June while you crooned our favorite toon" explanations of where romance comes from. One man we met in a marriage seminar wrote, "Romance is walking hand in hand on a moonlit beach with the wind blowing lightly in our faces—and our walk leading us back to our cottage where there awaits a fire, roses and satin sheets whispering our names."

But are these really the essential ingredients to stir up romance? If they are, what happens the next morning when our twosome begins to fuss over the wrinkles in the satin sheets as they make the bed, then haggle back and forth about who's going to take out the ashes from the fireplace or give more water to the drooping roses?

And if it takes "you and the night and the music" in order for romance to thrive, then it must be true that God has given us a mandate for marriage that's impossible for us to fulfill. He did, after all, declare in Ephesians 5 that marriage was to be a picture to the world of Christ's eternal romance with His bride, the Church. If the passionate partnership He wants for a man and wife always requires crackling fires, roses and satin sheets to survive, how can we possibly keep it alive in the harsh daylight when the mortgage payment is due on the ivy-covered cottage?

Where does romance come from, anyway?

The fire of romance that keeps Hallmark in business starts with a spark of "gimme." In other words, I'm attracted to a particular woman because of what she has to give me. Maybe I believe I'll finally feel important if someone as beautiful as this lovely woman will love *me*. Perhaps it's her warmth, or when she compliments me, that gives me a feeling of worth. Possibly her willingness to follow me gives me a sense of power or control. Or else her offer to lead me makes me feel secure. I may see winning her love as my chance to capture a lifetime supply of the companionship, or lovemaking, or encouragement I long for. Whatever the reason, I want her for what she can do for me. These qualities in her make me want to give myself to win her. That's when the fireworks and romance rockets explode across the sky!

Of course, there's a catch to this dynamic. If I married my wife because I wanted a 38–24–38 knockout to parade before my friends, but three pregnancies have changed the curves of her girlish figure, then I stop giving to her. And when I stop giving, our romance fades.

Or if the strong leadership she was promised during our courtship begins to look more like domineering bossiness, then *she* quits giving, and romance stops living.

What results is a story that sounds like this:

Nice night in June
Stars shine, big moon
In park with girl.
Heart pound, head swirl
Me say "Love . . ."; she coo like dove.
Me smart, me fast
Me not let chance pass
"Get hitched," me say.
She say, "Okay."
Wedding bells, ring, ring
Honeymoon, everything
Settle down, married life
Happy man, happy wife.
Another night in June

Stars shine, big moon
Ain't happy no more.
Carry baby, walk floor
Wife mad, she stew
Me mad, stew too.
Life one big spat
Nagging wife, bawling brat
Realize at last Me move too fast.

But we come bringing good news—no, *wonderful* news! Romance doesn't have to be fueled by "gimme" love. It can start with "serve-you" love, or what the Bible describes as a servant's heart. Observing this giving kind of love in action is what prompted me to write:

We believe a man and wife
Would have a better married life
If they would try out-serving one another.
For deeper love is felt
When what is done is not for self
But when it's done to satisfy the other.

Marriage isn't the act of choosing the one we'll *receive* from forever. It's selecting the one we'll *give to* for a lifetime. "Serve-you" love produces acts of giving that continue to stir up romance, whether great waves of mushy feeling come washing in with it or not.

The passion that arcs between Christ and His church has less to do with emotion than it does with a mutual decision to give ourselves in service to each other. Jesus explained to His disciples, "The Son of Man did not come to be served, but to serve" (Mark 10:45). Lasting romance begins when a husband and wife start viewing marriage as a chance to meet each other's needs. This love springs from a heart that's grateful for Christ's lavish service to us. Though it often results in the kind of electricity Hallmark would call romantic, it can continue to survive even when the rushing tides of emotion have ebbed.

Before Annie and I were married, a wise friend passed on this piece of advice: "Steve, let all that you do and say be a service to her. Pleasing *her* should be your highest priority. Take no concern for your own satisfaction. If you do this, you'll be blessed with a relationship that is not only full of joy, but also most pleasing to the Lord."

To be honest, I've not found my friend's advice the easiest to follow. But I will agree that as I've chosen to focus on Annie's needs, a servant's heart *in action* does generate romance at its best!

Maybe your marriage started on the wrong foot, like the man I heard about who pleaded with his girl friend, "Let's get married. I'm tired of being charming!" Even with a beginning as bad as that, you and your spouse can find yourselves, after five, ten, twenty or thirty years, enjoying the same freshness, love, respect and sense of adventure that newlyweds feel for each other. How? By learning to care for each other, listening to each other and meeting each other's changing needs. The romance doesn't have to wither. As a servant's heart replaces "gimme" love, your marriage can blossom and grow anew.

So, how do I get a servant's heart?

Daily life, its responsibilities and demands, does have a way of taking the steam out of you. Most men I know come home from a hard day at work and just want to relax. Because we feel as if we've been jumping all day to the demands of our boss, customers, fellow workers or the phone, we naturally feel as if we'd rather be left *alone*. And we forget that a woman's reaction to a tough day, or even a great day, is that she wants to share it with the man she loves. Who is going to make up the difference when this gap opens up?

Annie and I aren't marriage counselors. Nor are we psychologists or ordained ministers. But we are happily married. In the middle of a world where more than half the couples marrying will later decide to split up, we're together and growing. We're facing the same money pressures and job struggles and parenting hassles as others do—but we're pressing on and (most of the time!) enjoying the journey.

Of course we've uncovered our share of what looked like irreconcilable differences. But for the most part, we've found ways to turn those differences into reasons why we need each other more.

We want to help you find what we've found and, more than that, equip you to enjoy the particular romance God designed for you and your mate. Our guide? It's certainly not the world around us, where married men sport bumper stickers on their cars with slogans like "It used to be wine, woman and song. Now it's beer, the old lady, and television."

We're not simply drawing on the examples of other Christian couples, either. The expert we've consulted is better than these. He's available 'round the clock, understands us better than we do ourselves, has all wisdom, and wants to involve himself totally with us—all without making us feel foolish or guilty.

You've probably guessed, we're talking about Jesus.

Jesus doesn't expect us to pour out love from an empty bucket. He wants to fill our lives with His love, and from that fullness we can give. When Christ wanted to set a powerful example of service to His disciples, He drew on God's resource. The Scripture says, "Jesus, knowing that the Father had given all things into His hands, and that He had come forth from God and was going back to God,

humbled himself and washed the dirty feet of His follow-
ers" (John 13:3).

Jesus' needs were met by God. Therefore, He could
give unselfishly. As we look to Him to meet our needs,
we can then have all we require, plus the love we need to
serve our mates.

It doesn't take much to acquire a servant's heart, really.
First, we simply have to admit our need. Christ came to
heal the diseased, not those who are already whole. We
can't become eligible to receive His work in our hearts
unless we admit our selfishness and inability to change
ourselves into the givers we want to be.

Maybe you're not sure what a servant's heart looks
like because you've never seen one in action. Perhaps your
parents were not the best example of what it means to
love with selfless devotion.

If that's the case, we can still look to the greatest servant of all, Jesus, for a perfect model to follow. He served
us as He resisted temptation in order to live a sinless life.
He served us as He allowed himself to be brutally nailed
to a cross so He could redeem us. And He now serves us
in heaven as He intercedes for us with the Father. He can
show us how to serve, and then empower us to do it. All
we need to do is ask for His help.

If you admit your need and ask God to do surgery on
your selfishness, you can expect Him to say yes! He's
promised to never turn away those who seek Him. If you
commit yourself to serve your spouse in *God's* strength,
He will commit himself to help you. And help you He
will. You've chosen to align yourself with the design of
heaven when you decide to learn to give, so heaven will
align itself with you. God may reward your efforts by
changing your mate in ways that please you. Or He may
change *you* instead. Or both. In any case, you'll win, be-

cause when you give for Jesus' sake, He guarantees you will receive.

No matter how good—or bad—your marriage is today, you can begin at once to change for the better by learning to serve your spouse. Then you'll no longer need to ask, "Where did the romance go?"

> Some of you men, who are working hard
> Day after day, you come home tired.
> You got a good woman there, who's in love with
>   you,
> But do you realize what some of you are doing?
>
> You read the paper while the two of you eat
> No conversation while you watch TV,
> But when it's time to turn out the lights
> That's when you want to pay attention to your
>   wife.
>
> And it's making her feel like a stranger with you;
> It's making her feel like she's being used.
> She don't want to feel that way with you—
> Where did the romance go?
>
> Show her you love her all day long;
> Then loving in the night won't feel wrong.
> And oh, my brothers, don't you forget
> There's a whole lot more to love than just making
>   it.
>
> Don't make her feel like a stranger with you;
> Don't make her feel like she's being used.
> She don't want to feel that way with you—
> Where did the romance go?
> You better find it.
> Where did the romance go?[1]

---

[1]"Where Did the Romance Go?" Lyrics by Steve Chapman. © Copyright 1982 by Dawn Treader Music (SESAC). All rights reserved. International copyright secured. Used by permission of Gaither Copyright Management.

Who's the Boss?

ANNIE: When we got married, most of the Christian marriage formulas boiled down to one easy transaction: Man in Charge + Woman who Submits = Uninterrupted Bliss.

If you took this teaching to its extreme (which, sadly, *I* always seem to do with any good teaching), you find that a wife needs to have only two words in her vocabulary: "Yes" and "dear." But I was young and eager to please the Lord and my new husband. So I determined to "yes, dear" our way to happiness. We'd get ready for an evening out, and he'd say, "Where do you want to go?"

"Oh, anywhere *you* want to go, dear."

"Is there any special kind of food you are hungry for?"

"Oh, anything *you* want to eat, dear."

"Which of these two movies sounds better to you?"

"Whichever one *you'd* like to see, dear."

All right. It wasn't quite *that* bad, but you get the idea. This caricature of mindless submission I'd adopted is what led us to the Copperhead Confrontation.

In the days before our garage apartment (and if you had one of those, you'll remember it was the one without a washer and dryer!), we shared a farmhouse with two other couples. Be assured, we weren't doing this out of a great love for communal living. The farmhouse cost $100 a month, and only by splitting the rent three ways could we make the payment.

If the idea of farm living felt comfortable and romantic to me at the start, all the romance faded the day I found a snake in the yard. And *that* was the good news! The bad news was that the snake was a deadly poisonous copperhead. And where there was one, there was bound to be more.

Of course I yelled for Steve. He and his friend Ron came running and went after that snake, while I stayed on the porch and cheered for the great white hunters stalking their prey. Well, the snake was smarter than they were, and it eluded them at every turn. But then I saw it coming right toward *me*. I looked down, and saw that I was standing right over a small hole in the porch floor. Instantly, I realized the snake had taken up residence there and was headed back home. (Fortunately, it hadn't occurred to me yet that a whole pack of his nasty relatives might be right under my feet, or I would have been hysterical.) The snake, meantime, was slithering like sixty toward his hole in the porch. And Steve, realizing he was about to lose him yelled, "Grab that snake!"

Any sane woman would have burst out laughing at such a ridiculous idea and, instead, taken a flying leap *off* the porch. But not me. At the sound of my master's voice, all those months of teaching seized control of my faculties. "Tarzan say, 'Grab snake.' Me grab snake." And just as the copperhead started into the hole, I reached down and clamped onto him. He stiffened in my hand, and as I realized what I'd done, I screamed, tore back my arm and let him fly into the yard, where Steve and Ron promptly did him in.

Then Steve came stomping over, the color drained from his face. (He wasn't the only one!) "Annie! I can't believe you grabbed that snake," he said, wide-eyed.

"I can't believe you *asked* me to!" I choked out angrily.

That was the day we both decided we needed some balance in the way we came to our decisions. We weren't sure what the Lord wanted when He called for submission in marriage, but we knew it couldn't be this!

As we looked at the Scripture, we began to realize we'd overlooked an important truth. God called us "fellow heirs" of the grace of life (1 Pet. 3:7). He sees us as teammates, two people sharing a yoke, just like a team of oxen do, pulling *together* to get the job done. For a yoke of oxen to be effective, both have to be pulling part of the load. I'd been trying to make Steve carry the whole load, while I sat back passively and enjoyed the ride—except when I had to accept strange orders like "Grab that snake!"

Now, a yoke of oxen also only work well if they're headed the same direction. In our "do-your-own-thing" age, this kind of teamwork is especially hard to pull off. Every television sitcom, women's magazine, and talk show convinces us we've got to watch out for Number One. They tell us that a strong, happy person is one who holds tightly to independence, lest he be taken advantage of. How different this is from the teamwork model of New Testament marriage, where each partner seeks to "submit to [each other] out of reverence for Christ" (Eph. 5:21, NIV). The reason for Christian marriage isn't just so its participants will be happier, or less lonely, or more understood, though those benefits will surely be true of a marriage centered in God. Christian marriage was designed to honor Christ, so our fear of the Lord, and our reverence for Him motivates us to want to work as a team, for His glory.

Sometimes working as a team means I give up the way I want to do things. Sometimes it means dialoguing until my ideas fit together with my spouse's. Other times it means taking charge. Like the time Steve got an ear infection and refused to see the doctor.

When I say he had an infection, I'm understating the situation. Actually, he was so sick his eardrums burst and he was bleeding from his ears. There he lay, writhing in pain, but the man absolutely refused to see a doctor.

I listened to his moaning as long as I could. When I could stand it no longer, I called a specialist and explained his symptoms. The doctor agreed it was serious, and said, "It's closing time, but if you tell him to come in right now, I'll wait."

Unfortunately, this medical confirmation failed to overcome my husband's physician-phobia. He made no move to budge from his bed. I knew the time had come for drastic measures.

"Steve," I announced, "in First Corinthians it says a wife has rights over her husband's body. So those ears may be on your head, but they're *my* ears, too. And I'm taking my ears to the doctor. You can go with clothes, or without clothes . . . I don't care, but my ears are getting medical treatment."

Then I started pulling him out of bed. Steve was worse than a child. I could have carried a child to the car, but this 175-pounder—no way. So what I did was to begin prodding him out from under the covers.

Well, by now he saw there'd be no dissuading me. So he grumpily staggered out of bed, fumbled his way into a warm-up suit and dragged along to the doctor.

In the car on the way back home, I apologized for being so bossy. And when he forgave me, he also acknowledged

I'd helped him do what he knew he ought to do anyway. We drove home in peace. (By the way, "our" ears recovered completely.)

If authority is a shared effort, then what about the practical, everyday management of the home and family? Some people feel that the woman should be responsible for childrearing and housework, while the man should be the sole provider and the bearer of the heavier household tasks. Wouldn't it be nice if life were just that simple, if there were not so many gray areas?

How should the tasks be divided in a marriage? It depends, it seems to us, on what's best for the team effort to honor the Lord, and on how we can best serve each other.

With us, for example, Steve pays the monthly bills on a regular basis. We do it this way because I tend to operate in a general, idea-oriented mode, while Steve thinks more precisely. Generalities have their place, but balancing a checkbook isn't one of them; so to maintain our financial solvency, we agreed the bill-paying would be best done by Steve.

Just recently, however, when we purchased a different home I did the final negotiating with the realtor. That's because I thrive on resolving conflicts. I find it exhilarating to offer and counter-offer until an agreement is reached, but this process makes Steve uncomfortable.

So should the husband or wife handle the business end of family life? We believe it depends on each one's skills, as well as needs. Sometimes a task may shift from one to the other of us. This happens when the one who is usually responsible for a certain job is under particular pressure, or simply needs help.

For example, I normally do the grocery shopping, but if I'm overtaxed, Steve's been known to push a cart up and down the aisles for me. Likewise, I will help him shoulder one of his usual tasks when circumstances are pressing in on him.

Now, I believe completely in the trade-off system I just described. I do. But because marriage is a union of two imperfect people, it doesn't always work out quite so smoothly. Sometimes the things we care about, we don't easily let go of. And each partner doesn't always have the same idea of what's best for the team. Then what?

This was the question plaguing the Chapman household several Christmases ago. Because when it comes to Christmas, Steve becomes Scrooge, but I turn into Sister Claus. Hardly a workable combination!

You see, one of my dreams growing up was of an extravagant celebration at Christmas. The holidays I longed for looked like a reenactment of a Lennon Sisters' Christmas Special. There'd be a fire crackling, cookies baking, and the house would be elegantly ornamented, beribboned and swagged with evergreen boughs. Then you'd see my family, posed in a scene lovely enough to adorn a greeting card. We'd all be dressed to the teeth in velvet and plaid taffeta, and gathered around the piano singing carols in four-part harmony.

In my real family, though, no one played the piano. And with six kids, you'd never get the house *that* immaculate in the first place, let alone keep it that way long enough to belt out a chorus of "Hark, the Herald Angels Sing." And I've yet to see all eight members of my family in a good mood at the same time. So singing or no singing, we never could make this holiday fantasy come true. So I tucked away my dream for the days when I'd have my own home. Surely then I'd be able to celebrate the way I'd always hoped.

Steve also brought his own convictions to December 25. While I love everything about Christmas, Steve loathes everything about it except the birth of our Savior. And even that he celebrates with reservation, since he's quick to point out that December 25 wasn't actually the Lord's birthday, and he'll tell you how the choice of that date has pagan connotations.

So what happens to the glory of a smooth-working Christian marriage when the wife is Santa's helper, and the husband says, "No elves or reindeer allowed"?

Our first attempt at a solution was to *compromise* in an attempt to keep peace. Steve tried to avoid a row by letting me decorate a tree. That, I grudgingly agreed, was a real compromise, since he believed the whole idea of trees and ornaments was a pagan custom that shouldn't be part of a believer's Christmas. And he allowed me to buy gifts for the children—another tough compromise since he thought all this gift-giving simply taught them materialism and greed.

I tried to inject the season with what celebrating I could without offending him—and felt sorry for myself the whole time. Okay, so we had a tree, but it never would have made it at the Lennon Sisters' house. It was a dreadful aluminum thing that I picked up at a garage sale. (The box was marked $1.00, but the lady didn't put up any resistance when I offered less. So you have an idea how charming this tree really was.) And to decorate it, I baked sugar cookies with paper-clip hangers in the end, because I figured buying ornaments would send my husband into a tailspin. The kids did get gifts, but, at Steve's insistence, only one apiece.

Both of us were trying to get what we could of our own way. And make no mistake, both of us were sure we were also doing what was best for the team. Steve felt he needed to hold firm because he was saving our kids from worldliness. I believed we needed all this celebrating to make the birth of our Lord one of the high points of our year as a family. And each of us could have made a highly persuasive, and even spiritual-sounding case for why we were right. So there was no open warfare, but our differing view of Christmas was *not* something we joked about with others. Neither of us saw much that was funny in the other's stubbornness.

An uneasy truce reigned—until one snowy Christmas morning. The kids had opened their one gift from us, and then unwrapped the few others that family and compassionate neighbors had provided. When the last one had been ripped open, one of them looked up and asked, "Where's the rest of it?"

With that innocent question, Hurricane Steve unleashed its fury. He rose to his feet, with holy fire ablazin' in his eyes, and thundered into his favorite sermon on the evils of Christmas.

Eventually, he ran out of steam. I'm sure these kinds of sermons are more enjoyable to preach when you have an eager audience shouting "Amen" and "You tell 'em, brother." I assure you Steve received no such encouragement from his captive congregation of three. So, Steve stopped pacing and waving his finger in the air, and returned to his chair to open *his* gifts. The rest of us retreated to our rooms.

Steve and I didn't talk for the rest of the day. I was hurt and angry, and more so as the day wore on. I felt I'd sacrificed major slabs of my holiday dream for this man. And instead of being appreciated, I'd gotten a lecture. I realized, too, that any hopes I still cherished for having a picture-pretty Christmas would have to die. Steve was *not* going to budge an inch on this issue.

Steve, meanwhile, was rumbling around with his own set of angry reactions. And that night we violated the Scripture and let the sun go down on our wrath. I lay in bed crying while he had the gall to curl up next to me and go to sleep. But was he really asleep? I wasn't convinced.

He made some half-baked attempts at fake snoring, though. And he even offered that "I'm-falling-into-a-deep-sleep-now" jerk. He didn't have to go that far, though. The word jerk was already going through my mind!

The next morning we got into the car for the full-day's drive to our parents' homes in West Virginia. As we prepared to go and "share the joy," our anger was in full force. Neither of us was willing to yield our wills to the Holy Spirit and take a step toward healing.

Seven hours of frozen fury followed. And it wasn't until we crossed the border of West Virginia, about thirty miles from our destination, that Steve broke the silence. He admitted later that his initiative was not motivated by great remorse, but by the embarrassment he knew he'd feel if his parents saw us acting like this.

"Annie, we have to have a conversation about our conflict."

From between clenched teeth I replied icily, "I'm listening."

So Steve had a conversation about our conflict.

"I guess I've been a jerk about this whole Christmas thing," he began tentatively.

"I know you have." No thaw in sight.

"Do you think we can patch this riff between us so that we can go to our parents' and have a nice Christmas?" he asked.

"The prospects of us having a nice Christmas are questionable," I returned, "but I'm willing to be civil to your family while we're visiting them."

This initial interchange could go down in our personal history as the worst example of loving cooperation. And we were pushed to it mostly by our pride. But after years of marriage, we've learned to be grateful for anything that forces us to begin to work out the hard stuff.

During the next two days we talked off and on about

Christmas. We threw out this solution and that. But each of them finally turned into a power struggle between us. Anger and hurt feelings made the issue of *who* would be right more important than *what* was right. It appeared we'd never find a middle ground.

So I decided to give. "Steve," I said slowly, "for years I've tried hard to make Christmas special for our family, but I've failed. So I'm giving you the freedom to make our Christmas into whatever you want. I won't push for anything, or do anything at all about Christmas unless you ask me to."

It's hard to express what a difficult thing this decision was for me. I felt Steve had proved himself unworthy of placing my trust in him when it came to Christmas. So to entrust him with *my* Christmas came as easily as would handing one of my children over to a mad gorilla. I realized I could well be opening myself to spend next December 25 in a cheerless, giftless (but totally unmaterialistic) "celebration." But I realized that insisting on my way had resulted in division between Steve and me. And it was bringing dishonor to the Lord, who wanted our marriage to be an example of the way love and unity flow between Christ and His church. I knew the Lord wanted me to give up my Christmas dream for His sake.

And even though Steve had disappointed me about the holiday, I reviewed *all* I knew of him. His Christmas Scroogery wasn't motivated by selfishness. He really was concerned for our family—even if we had different ideas about what was best for us. If he was wrong in this decision, so what? One day out of 365 wasn't going to ruin our life, or our children's lives. Steve was so loving and good, never stingy. Surely I could give that in return for all he gave us the rest of the year. I did love Christmas, but I decided I loved God—and the man God had given me—more. So the holiday was now in the hands of Steve

Chapman; Steve Chapman was in the hands of the Lord; and I was at peace.

Interestingly, without giving me one clue, the Lord was already doing some work on Steve. Not long before, Steve had attended a men's conference where the speaker taught from Malachi 2 about the terrible consequences of wounding your wife's spirit. Such an act, the speaker emphasized, could cut off a man's communication with God.

Steve realized that the tremendous disappointment I expressed about our holiday was really the outpouring of a wounded spirit. He told me later it stirred the fear of God in his heart. If shielding our kids from the stirring of greed resulted in wounding his wife, he knew it couldn't be right before God. Then, when I told him I was going to trust him to make the right decision about our holiday, the power struggle between us dissolved. So he was free to consider what might be best for all of us.

When the next December arrived, I stuck to my commitment to leave Christmas with Steve. Since he'd made no requests of me, I'd done no shopping, or decorating. Our halls may not have been decked with boughs of holly (or, in our case, boughs of tacky aluminum), but the tension we'd felt before wasn't there, either.

Then one evening, Steve and the kids pulled on hats, coats and boots and trooped out to the car without inviting me along. I busied myself with cleaning up the kitchen and paid little attention. When they returned, a couple hours later, Steve called from outside the front door—"Annie, come here a minute."

When I opened the door, there he stood, holding a *live* Christmas tree. The children stood glowing at his side. I stepped out of the way as they carried in boxes of decorations, lights, a centerpiece for the table, candles and even a tape of Christmas carols. We put on the carols, and decorated that beautiful, fragrant tree. Steve made a fire and

I started a batch of cookies. . . . It was a scene fit to make the Lennon Sisters die of envy!

And it's been repeated every year since.

I don't want you to get the idea my man did a total turnaround. He insists on holding up the decorations and asking the Lord to sanctify "these pagan items" before we put them on the tree—half out of conviction, I think, and half out of orneriness. And the children still only get one gift. But we shop for Christmas together now. It's no longer me sneaking around trying to do Christmas my way, or Steve sitting back sulking, wanting Christmas his way. Because we each chose to give to the other, out of reverence for Christ, it's the time of genuine celebration God intended.

What was important to us was the lesson we learned. Real submission has to start with submission to Christ. Marital decisions aren't a see-saw, with husband at one end and wife at the other. There is always a third, an overriding will to consider—what does the Lord want done here? We have to first submit to Him, and then listen. Thus there's no struggle left, except to find what He wants.

We all come into marriage with expectations—some we're aware of, and some we're not. If communication and compromise result in these expectations being met, that's wonderful. In most cases that is likely to happen. But sometimes deferring to each other may cost a great deal. And I know my Christmas dream was a small one compared to those others hold dear. But when we choose to submit, or defer, to our partner, it must be out of reverence for *Christ*. We do it as an act of giving to *Him*, not because we expect something back from our mate.

Sometimes when we give our dream to God, He gives it back, as He did with my holiday desires. Other times, He may change us so that desire isn't as important to us as it once was. And still other times, He may give us more of himself—His peace, His grace, His power—and that's the richest return of all. God is no one's debtor, and when we give to Him by deferring to our mate, He promises He will give back to us in greater measure than we ever gave.

The question of who'll be boss of the marriage partnership can turn every minor marital decision into a major struggle for control. But Christ intended He be the boss of our life together. When we serve Him by serving and giving to our mate, He'll improve the state of our union as we walk together in Him.

State of the Union

Madam, at this time, I submit to you
The terms of my report, the facts of my review.
You've heard it all before
You know what's on my mind
But still I think it's good to say from time to time:

This is my State of the Union message;
It is a message of a love set free.
I see the more you have given yourself to God
The more you have left for me.
I see the more you have given yourself to God
The more you have left for me.

Sir, in my reply, I would like to say
I'm also making notes; I watch you every day.
And from my report, I only can conclude
That what you see in me, I also see in you.

This is my State of the Union message;
It is a message of a love set free.
I see the more you have given yourself to God
The more you have left for me.
I see the more you have given yourself to God
The more you have left for me.[1]

Getting Rid of the Excess Baggage

ANNIE: *My name is Annie, and I am a Packaholic.*

If there were an organization for Compulsive Over-packers—that is, people who must pack everything they own in a suitcase each time they travel—I'd be their Woman of the Year.

I know, I know. Any person who has traveled full time the last fourteen years with a family of four *should* have packing down to an exact science. I certainly should have learned by now how to fit a month's worth of clothes into two carryons and a guitar case. But that's simply not how it is.

It's not that I don't try. I make lists, coordinate outfits and thrash myself mentally for all the things we took last time and wound up not needing. But when it comes time to actually stuff the suitcases, all my careful control goes *ka-plooey*. In go the ten purses and ten matching pairs of shoes, not to mention a complete assortment of clothing alternatives in case we hit cold weather, or hot weather, or rain, or a formal affair, or a casual get-together. On it goes. And this just for a weekend!

We leave loaded down with a humiliatingly inordinate amount of excess baggage. Just ask Steve, who serves as our overloaded luggage-handler. One day I hope I'll learn.

It's possible to come into marriage with excess baggage as well. And I'm not talking about Samsonite suitcases. The baggage burdening us may be wounds from the past, hurts and memories that keep us bound and unable to move ahead with our mate on the journey toward marital intimacy.

Steve and I hear of these wounds continually as we minister to people. Often, we receive letters from men and women all across the country who suffer deeply from the scars of a painful past.

If you are plagued by any of these scars, you may find some of their stories hard to take. Sometimes, just admitting that you *have* wounds can cause great pain. But it is vital to your spiritual and emotional growth that you identify these hurts, because Christ cannot heal suffering we insist isn't there. And without His healing, the weight of this excess baggage will drain away your joy and wreak havoc on your capacity to love and be loved.

The Baggage of Abuse

One young woman from Texas wrote, sharing this painful story:

> When I was a child, there were many nights that I would lie awake, wondering [how long it would be before] the lights came on. And then I'd hear my mother yell, "Harold, stop hitting me!" And I'd lie in bed with tears in my eyes, waiting for the moment when my mother would come rushing into the bedroom, to hurry all us children

out of bed to flee from daddy.

Another woman wrote:

> I come from a home of two alcoholic parents,
> [and] five children, of whom I'm the oldest. There
> was every abuse you can imagine in our home. . . .
> I have discovered during the last few years that all
> three of my brothers were being abused by my
> mother and that they, like my sister and I, were so
> caught up in what we thought was OUR fault that
> we didn't tell anyone.

The statistics are mind-boggling: One of every three
girls, and one of every six boys will be sexually molested
by the time they reach age eighteen. And it isn't just children who are forced to carry the baggage of abuse. You
may be a wife, or even a husband, who has suffered the
agony of physical or verbal battering from your marriage
partner. Studies say that one of two women is battered at
some time in her life. Four to five million have been hurt
badly. And the abuse happens at the same rate to people
of all income levels and religions.

Perhaps you may have been abused, even though your
partner is a Christian. In her book *Conjugal Crime*, Terry
Davison tells of growing up in a home where her father
beat her mother, yet he was a Christian minister! At
church he spoke respectfully of the things of God—but at
home he behaved brutally, sometimes spewing out verbal
or physical abuse just before or after saying grace at the
table.

A woman in just such a situation recently wrote us,
saying:

> My marriage is in terrible trouble. I am a Chris-
> tian and so is my husband, even though you would
> never know it by his actions right now. My hus-

band degrades me constantly and verbally abuses me in many ways. He tells me all the problems that we have are all my fault. I am trying to serve the Lord and keep the family together, but it's really hard. I realize that [when] marriages fall apart, the children are the broken pieces, and I don't want my children to be broken pieces. I don't know how much more I can stand.

Abuse is not the only thing that can weigh us down, of course. There are other types of baggage, like neglect.

The Baggage of Neglect

God intended that in our first family we'd see His loving care. Steve, for instance, has many wonderful memories of his father. I'll let him tell it.

STEVE: I clearly recall the times my father would drive our family through the hills of West Virginia. I'd be standing right behind him in the car, with my chin planted on Dad's shoulder. Now I think about the sight my father would glimpse in the rearview mirror. I was seven years old, awkward and pretty sickly-looking. My teeth went in all directions, and a serious illness had left me with a skinny body and dark circles under my eyes. Probably my dad could see he'd never be able to sit on the bleachers and cheer as his boy blasted fifty yards for a touchdown.

But, even knowing full well what his son might never be, he'd still say to me, "Steve, let's you and me talk." He'd take one hand off the wheel, reach back and gently pat the back of my head. And we'd talk—about everything and nothing.

ANNIE: Now, that's what God intended parents to do for their children. But it may not have been the experience in your home. As one young woman wrote:

My father took very little interest in my life as I was growing up. Because of the business my parents were in, they had no time for me or for a normal family life. They did the best they could, but I grew up feeling terribly insecure.

When I was about twelve years old I began being noticed by boys. By my mid-teens, I was involved with men much older than I. It seemed I was always looking for men who looked like my dad.

I married young, after having become involved with a young man physically. I felt so guilty and knew what I was doing was wrong. Two children later—we divorced. I know now I was just looking for my daddy's love.

The Baggage of Anger Toward Those Who Hurt Our Loved Ones

A young parent wrote:

I am a single parent. My husband informed me that what he wanted to do in life did not include a wife and kids. So, since the summer of 1986, the kids and I have been on our own. I have two great kids—a girl and a boy ages 6 and 5. I am sure the divorce has really affected both of them. . . .

This woman went on to say that she did not know how to get free of the gnawing anger at her husband. For, daily she had to live with the pain and loss she saw on the faces of her two dear children.

The Baggage of Broken Relationships

Broken friendships can load you down, so that all your relationships are affected:

Two people whom I work with and I trust deeply hurt me in a way I don't know how to explain. They betrayed me and I felt so rejected that I kept getting more and more depressed until I actually tried to commit suicide.

Or the breakdown may be between you and your spouse.

My husband and I are now separated; we were married for nearly twenty years. He says he loves me, but I don't know if I can trust him. We are separated because he wants to go out with other women.

He says he is sorry and that he wants us to have another chance. I don't know if I can go through all this again. This has happened before. I have left him a number of times. I don't know why, but I still love him. Do you believe marriages are made in heaven? I used to think ours was till all these troubles came. I just don't know if we can have trust again.

And it isn't just women who know this kind of heartbreak.

Will you please pray for me and my family? My wife and I married nearly twenty years ago. We divorced last year, and were remarried six months later. Now we are headed for the divorce courts again. We have four beautiful children and my heart is aching.

My parents divorced as I was going into adolescence. At that time pornography got a hook in my jaw. Even though I received Christ as my Savior at age eighteen (largely through my wife's influence), the roots of this sin were not dealt with. We felt a call to the ministry, went to Bible college, served in the pastorate for ten years and also worked in other Christian services. All this time I lived with guilt and a sense of hypocrisy due to periodically, yet regularly, yielding to this insatiable lust of the flesh. As one thing led to another, I eventually became unfaithful physically, as well as mentally. When my wife learned of it she was destroyed.

The last five years have been unbelievable. To make a long story short, she is emotionally dead toward me today and says that she does not want to try to make our marriage work anymore. I feel totally responsible.

The Baggage of Wrong Choices

So far, we've looked at problems that others place on us. Sometimes, though, we feel weighed down by our own mistakes.

After one concert a shy, young woman of about eighteen came and stood nearby as I talked with some other people. Finally, after everyone had left, I turned to her. It was then I saw the deep, relentless sorrow in her eyes. "Is there something on your mind, honey?"

"The baby would be a year old now, if . . . I hadn't had the abortion. . . ." She said she was a Christian, and told me she believed bearing a child out of wedlock would hurt her Christian testimony. She'd felt she had no other choice.

I asked her if anyone at the clinic had prepared her for the feelings of loss, regret, and mourning for the child that they had torn from her body.

"*No!*" she replied. "If I had known it was going to be like this . . . Oh, God . . . I wouldn't have done it. I just sit and hold my Cabbage Patch doll and cry."

The jagged scars on her wrist and lower arm made it clear she'd attempted other ways to end her sorrow as well.

The Way Out

Scripture portrays marriage as two people becoming one, uniting spiritually, emotionally, and physically in one love and one purpose. But it's not difficult to see how much harder this uniting becomes when one or both of the partners still writhes in pain from wounds in the past. These wounds keep a couple from settling into the oneness God wants for them.

Recently we moved, but we weren't able to sell our first home before we had to leave it. All during the time our first house hadn't sold, we were never able to feel settled in the new location. The unfinished business of an unsold house kept us from feeling free to rest peacefully elsewhere.

As we talked about this, Steve mused, "Do you suppose it works the same for marriages? Do wounds from the past keep people from settling in and feeling at home in their marriage?"

Indeed! Coming together loaded down with life's excess baggage is about as easy as a man and woman trying to make love with fifteen suitcases between them.

But it is possible to find healing from these wounds. And it comes by forgiving the one who has wounded you.

Ouch! That wasn't what you wanted to hear, was it? And I know from experiences in my own life how very, *very* difficult forgiving a person can be, especially when you've been hurt so deeply again and again.

But I don't apologize when I insist that you must forgive the one (or ones) who've hurt you. Because I believe

God's Word teaches there's *no other way* to healing, except by the surgical removal of bitterness with the knife of forgiveness.

Jesus insisted on it. He told His disciples to pray, "Forgive us our debts, *as we have forgiven our debtors*" (Matt. 6:12).

Scripture doesn't record that any of the disciples argued out loud with Him about His strict stand on forgiveness. But He must have known they were arguing mentally because He went on to say, "For if you forgive men when they sin against you, your heavenly Father will also forgive you. But if you do not forgive men their sins, your Father will not forgive your sins." Christ requires that we pardon those who've hurt us if we expect to receive pardon from God for our wrongdoing.

And here's the good news. When we choose to forgive, we're writing our own ticket to freedom. One woman, whose father sexually abused her during most of her childhood, once said to me, "I won't be free of his influence until he dies." But even his death will not set her free, because she's bound to this man and his evil by bonds of bitterness that even death can't break. She believes it's the abuse that is ruining her life, but I don't agree. Though she's been terribly wounded, God's power and grace is more than sufficient to heal her—even to bring beauty and strength despite this terrible violation. But when and if she chooses to respond to her abuser with forgiveness rather than bitterness, she will begin the trek toward spiritual health and freedom.

One thing needs to be made clear. We don't forgive those who've hurt us because they *deserve* it. We forgive only because Christ has forgiven us. We have no choice but to pass on the same grace to those who have wronged us. That's why Paul tells us, "Get rid of all bitterness, rage and anger . . . forgiving each other, *just as in Christ God forgave you*" (Eph. 4:31–32, NIV).

And when we forgive, we're certainly not saying that our abuser was right in what he or she did. We're not letting them off the hook. We're not whitewashing evil behaviors, renaming them "weaknesses," or "unfortunate choices," or "mistakes." Look back over the baggage we've described already. A father who terrorizes his little children . . . a spouse who commits adultery . . . a friend who betrays—these acts aren't just "problems"; they are downright *evil*. They need to be called what they are—sin—without denial or covering up.

But sin must be forgiven. We need to pardon the offender for Jesus' sake, for their sake, and also for our *own* sake. Bitterness that's allowed to take root and grow in you will have no effect on your abuser. But it will cripple you, and if allowed to continue, it can eventually snuff out your very life.

One woman who'd been violently molested said,

> Whenever I thought about forgiving this person who violated me so cruelly, I could not let that hurt go because he deserved to pay. The truth is, my thoughts of hatred and bitterness had absolutely no effect on him, but they were tearing my life apart.

This woman suffered crippling arthritis, broken relationships, and immense depression, which didn't begin to change until she decided that with God's help, she would begin actively to forgive her offender. She said,

> If I had a thought of hatred for this man—and I had many—I'd acknowledge the thought (not deny it), and then I would thank the Lord for how it would drive me to God.
>
> Then I would concentrate on God's love, and

His ability to forgive *me* no matter what I had done. I especially worked on thinking of Scripture passages that helped me focus on God's truth—like 1 John 4:7 that says, "Dear friends, let us love one another, for love comes from God." It helped me to choose to forgive this man.

After all this, I would pray for his salvation, and then ask God to give me divine forgiveness from my heart. It seemed I had to go through the same process a hundred times a day for a while. But after I relinquished my hatred, God did a real healing in my life.

The crippling arthritis has left my body. No longer am I victimized by the severe pain. God, in His infinite love and mercy, brought into my life the most precious man ever born, a man of godly character who loves me in purity and respect. We have been married for over ten years and have three beautiful children. We have had no trouble in communicating our mutual love sexually. In fact, I believe God has blessed us in an extra abundance in that area of our marriage because of the pain of the past. He, and He alone, can bring life from death, beauty from ashes. And that's what He's done in my life.

Does this lady's experience sound too good to be true? Scores of those who write to us would say "No!" Because they've found the same freedom she did when they chose the way of forgiveness.

Listen to just a few of their testimonies:

> I've been able to forgive my father and I've learned to go to God to supply my needs as my "heavenly Father." I no longer have to seek men to

fill that role in my life, for God has filled that longing. . . .

Through prayer I have lost the bitterness I had
toward my ex-husband. I have forgiven him. A cri-
sis occurred [when he abandoned our family]. But
we have survived and are actually better for having
gone through it. . . .

Even though I went through a really hard time,
I finally was able to allow God to heal me of feelings of rejection and the bitterness that went with
it. I [now] believe God works all things for the good
to them that love Him. Through my state of depression He has blessed me greatly. My husband and I
are closer than ever. I still have some bad days, but
I'm trusting the Lord to help me overcome my
problems. I am taking one day at a time, and I know
that I'm going to be all right, thanks to God. . . .

And for some, the one they needed to forgive was
themselves. You might forgive others, but never let yourself go free. Pardoning yourself is just as essential to finding
peace as forgiving any other person who has wronged you.

We've also received many messages of hope from
those who had to make this important step:

I had an abortion in 1972. Even though I knew
I was forgiven by God, I had not forgiven myself
or my husband for what we had done. We were
not married yet and I didn't want to hurt Christian
family members by me being pregnant—so we
chose abortion (which is a decision we wish now
we had not made!). That night after we talked I
forgave myself and my husband and he forgave me

and himself. That was a new beginning for our marriage. . . .

After having gone through a divorce, and having lived apart from the Lord during that time, I had a lot of guilt cluttering up my heart. I couldn't let go of it, even though I knew I had been forgiven. But I finally let Jesus in my "secret place." And after letting go of that guilt, I wanted to run and jump and shout for joy! For the first time I felt as if I was whole again, and able to hold my head up and be proud that Jesus loves me, a terrible sinner. I felt like such a failure because I had a failed marriage in my past. While some of my past is certainly nothing to be proud of, I could be proud of the fact that Jesus forgave me, died for me, and loves me still. . . .

Are you struggling under the load of excess baggage? Let Christ set you free from bondage to the wounds of the past. He wants you to know a satisfying *today*, and an even brighter *tomorrow*. He came to set captives free. Allow Him to liberate you so you can be free to love.

Two Children

Two children, a brother and a sister
Born to a father who was a slave to wine.
They do remember their younger years of
    sorrow,
How their daddy used to hurt them time after
    time.

But somehow they grew to be so different.
Their lives turned out to be like day and night.
One lives in peace up in Ohio;
One was full of hate until she died.

I wondered what could make the difference in
    the two of them.
Both had reasons to be bitter, but one was so
    sweet.
How could one live in peace and not the other?
Not long ago the answer came clear to me.

I saw the brother at his daddy's grave;
Placing flowers there his eyes were filled with
    tears.
He said, "Daddy, once again I do forgive you
For the way you made us suffer through the
    years."

Now I can see how the two could be so different,
How their hearts turned out to be like day and
    night.
He lives in peace up in Ohio;
She was bitter till the day she died.

He lives in forgiveness up in Ohio;
She was bitter till the day she died.
A bitter heart was the reason that she died.[1]

[1]"Two Children." Lyrics by Steve and Annie Chapman. © Copyright 1986 by Dawn Treader Music (SESAC). All rights reserved. International copyright secured. Used by permission of Gaither Copyright Management.

Irritations

STEVE: If you want to reduce a boulder to rubble, you could stuff a dozen sticks of dynamite under it, and let 'er blow.

Or, you could put a kid armed with a little hammer next to that boulder and let him *tap, tap, tap* on it. Give that kid about enough time and you'd find him sitting next to a pile of powder every bit as fine as the dynamite produced.

The same principle works in marriage. There are as many homes disintegrated by the *rat-a-tat-tat* of unresolved irritations as by the dynamite blast of an affair or alcoholism or abuse. Don't you know couples who wound up divorcing over her purchase of a coffee table, or his decision to take a fishing vacation? I do. But it wasn't the furniture or the fishing lures that broke them up.

Those, of course, were just the final irritations in a long, long string of differences that never got resolved. You see, it's not the differences themselves, but what we *do* about our differences—large *and* small—that will decide our marital destiny. For if you can't settle the Battle of the Toothpaste Tube, you surely won't be able to negotiate your way through the major war zones of marriage, the ones like sex, or money, or in-laws, or childrearing.

Every couple has differences. Speaking personally, I find many of the differences between Annie and me delightful! They constitute several of the reasons I married her. For instance, because of her talent for decorating, she's made our house into a lovely home. Me, I was never much for fussing with details like pictures on the walls or doo-dads on the mantel. In fact, before I married Annie, my definition of a well-kept bedroom was one where I threw all my dirty clothes into just one corner. (After we were married, Annie informed me that the four posts on our bed were *not* put there to be mannequins. They'd looked so convenient, sticking up like that, I'd just pick one and undress beside it. So all four of them were fully clothed at any given time.)

In light of my housekeeping handicap, you can imagine my pleasure as a newlywed when I came home to a place where the flower boxes had things growing in them and the refrigerator *didn't*!

There was, however, a side to Annie's decorating gift I wasn't prepared for. All that pretty paper adorning the walls . . . it doesn't just appear there by itself. The stuff has to be measured and cut and matched and pasted and rehung. There I'd be, hanging from a ladder trying to position an eight-foot strip of this wet, gooey paper straight on the wall—and at the same time, trying to match it up to the teeny-tiny flowers on the last piece, which were, of course, only about as big as good-sized fly specks. And just as I was getting the last strip glued down flat, I'd hear from down below, "This looks so wonderful. Why don't we do Heidi's room, too!"

(I know a woman who insists if God hadn't intended

divorce, He never would have invented wallpaper. There are days I've wondered if maybe she doesn't have a point.)

I discovered, also, that just because Annie's furniture arrangements looked great, that didn't mean she intended them to stay that way. Like the true artist she is, Annie always insists that perfect can be made more perfect, which, of course, necessitates constant change.

Today, the teacups may be in the dining room hutch. Tomorrow, they may have been moved to the kitchen. I can never expect to walk into a darkened room in our house and plunk into my recliner, because in the time it took me to go out for a newspaper, Annie may have decided the living room grouping needed the recliner more than the family room did. Heaven help me if I ever go blind and have to find my way around our house! A trip across the living room would leave me with severe shin fractures! You wonder where the expression "Here today, gone tomorrow" came from? I'm sure the writer came up with it while watching Annie in her decorating mode.

Of course, Annie could come up with her own Jeckel and Hyde stories of our differences. She says one of the things she loved about me when we were dating was the aura of excitement I always exuded. Physical dangers scare her more than they do me, so she loved my masculine daring.

No one told her, of course, that this "masculine daring" causes me to push a tank of gas just as far as it will go. It's Man against Meter, so the closer I come to lurching into the gas station with nothing left in the tank but fumes, the more I feel like a winner.

In my own defense, I have never actually run out of gas. Not long ago, however, I came the closest I ever have. We left home early for a Sunday morning concert, and we were on the highway before I realized I had never before seen that gas gauge *that* far below empty. And because we'd left so early, I knew no gas stations would be open yet. But I also knew we couldn't go a half mile on what was left in that tank. So we were either going to have to chance getting stalled on the highway, or stop right then at a station I could see ahead and wait for it to open.

I did pull into the station but, too proud to admit the gauge had "bested" me this time, I cheerily announced to my family we were going to "stop here and rest a bit." The "bit" turned out to be forty-five minutes, until the manager arrived to pump us some gas. My family wasn't fooled in the slightest by my "resting" routine.

I pull these same kinds of stunts when we get lost on a trip. We're not sure where we are, and suddenly it becomes Man against the Wilderness, and it's up to me to find a way through that maze of freeways and bring my little family safely home. Stop and ask for directions? Did Lewis and Clark stop at a Standard station? Would Davy Crockett have called AAA? The adrenalin starts pumping, my hands tighten on the steering wheel, and we strike out to make it all on our own.

Annie insists, however, we never heard Mrs. Crockett's side of the story. How many church suppers did she have to walk into late because Davy wouldn't ask directions? And how many times did she find herself without horsepower because Davy insisted on seeing how far their old nag could go without food?

Differences. *Every* couple has them. And the ones we most loved when we first came together are usually the same ones that later force a wedge between us. That's why it matters that we learn *how* to deal with these differences so our marriage doesn't get irritated to death.

Irritations: Say It With Love

To settle our irritations, we always begin by applying a truth so obvious that when I say it you're going to wonder if I'm a parolee from the Indiana State Home for the Dense. But I'm going to say it anyway: Your partner has to know how he or she is irritating you before any change can take place. So, if you're irritated, *say so.*

I told you it would sound obvious. But you'd be surprised at the people we meet to whom this isn't so obvious. We know lots of women who believe the Bible's challenge to submit to their husbands means they should never voice any displeasure or irritations or disagreement. If they do, they're swamped with guilt for acting so unsubmissively.

Others we know won't bring up their gripes because they believe God wants them to be "peacekeepers." But Jesus never told us to *keep* the peace; instead, we're to be peace*makers.* Peace*keepers* avoid conflict at any cost. But peacemakers take an honest look at differences, and seek ways to come to mutually acceptable terms of resolution. To a peacekeeper, conflict is the enemy. To a peacemaker, conflict simply presents an opportunity to communicate and compromise so both sides can do a better job of understanding and giving to each other.

When I married Annie, I asked her to be sure she always told me when something in our life displeased her. She's been faithful to do that, and I've been glad. Like many men, I'm not very sharp in threading my way through the intricacies of emotional communication. (I do remember one time I asked Annie if something was wrong. She said no, and I had the good sense to not accept her answer. Of course when she insisted everything was all right, her voice was as flat as three-day-old ginger ale, and the look on her face would have made a death-row inmate look happy by comparison. I may be slow, but no one's *that* slow!) For the most part, I knew I'd need help to know if things weren't right.

But because she's told me how she felt, I know my

antics with our auto fuel bother her. I know we don't agree on how the toilet paper should be inserted on the roller, and that it makes her crazy when I leave my beard trimmings in the sink. (She tells me it looks as if our sink is growing hair—gray hair at that. I have to agree that thought is pretty disgusting!)

But when she expresses an irritation, she makes it easier for me to hear because she's also faithful to practice three "nevers."

She never couples her irritation with *character assassination.* For instance, she never says things like, "What kind of *slob* would leave half his beard in the sink?"

She never makes her complaint *a moral judgment,* holding her nose in the air and saying, "I'm sure a really *godly* husband wouldn't get us lost like this at 11:30 at night."

And she never *insists her solution is the only way to resolve our difference.*

When she comes to me with an irritation, it's usually in a spirit like this: "Steve, when you leave your clothes in the middle of the floor, I feel as though I'm expected to be a slave. I feel taken for granted. Now, tell me how you see it, and let's work this out together." She keeps her complaint to just one issue, and makes it clear how deeply it bothers her; but she also practices the kind of love that "doesn't insist on its own way." She gives me a chance to work with her toward a mutually agreeable solution.

And she makes me want to work toward a solution, because she's as quick (actually, quicker) to point out what she *likes* about me, and how I *please* her, as she is to voice irritations.

Please don't get the idea that sniffing out conflicts is the woman's job in a marriage. It certainly isn't. But as I said earlier, Annie seems to have a relational seismograph that picks up rumbles between us that I wouldn't feel until they became a quake big enough to flatten half of San

Francisco. And I believe many women share that capacity.

But the three "nevers" work equally well whether husband or wife is the irritated one. Using them while you let your partner hear your beef can keep a minor dogfight from escalating into World War III. It can help you get the coffee-table conflicts out on the table, and lead you to resolving them before they get so big you wind up dividing up all the rest of the furniture in a divorce settlement.

When the Other Ship Won't Budge

The place where we've starting talking about irritations sounds good, doesn't it? You simply, in a calm and gracious manner, voice your concern to your partner, and together you find a solution you're both happy with. That works great . . . part of the time. But if you believe that's how it's always going to be, I have news you aren't going to like. Sometimes your partner simply isn't going to change.

It reminds me of the story of a captain piloting his ship through dark and stormy waters. Up ahead he spotted what he thought was the light of another ship headed right toward him.

He grabbed the ship's loudspeaker and bellowed into it, "Collision imminent. Veer ten degrees north!"

But back across the dark waters a voice replied, "No, *you* veer ten degrees south."

"I am an admiral," the first man said. "Now, veer ten degrees north."

"I'm just a midshipman," the voice in the dark returned, "but you still must veer ten degrees south."

Now the light ahead was dangerously close. "This is a *battleship*," the captain said, as menacingly as he could. "Now veer ten degree north."

"You veer ten degrees south," the voice said evenly,

"because *this* is a lighthouse."

Sometimes the behaviors that irritate us aren't going to change . . . maybe not now, maybe never. (Annie could illustrate this point for you, if you're not sure what I mean. You see, just last week I nearly ran out of gas again. . . .)

So, what's a body to do with an irritation that doesn't just go away?

You've probably heard the prayer by Francis of Assissi that goes like this:

> Lord, grant me the serenity
> to accept the things I cannot change,
> the courage to change the things I can,
> and the wisdom to know the difference.

The things we can't change about our mate, we have to accept if we're to have peace.

Acceptance isn't the same as resignation. You can recognize resignation when you hear the sounds of pitiful pouting, and the moans of martyrdom. ("He treats me so bad [*sigh*]. But I married him, so I guess I have to put up with it.")

Acceptance comes easier when you don't expect perfection of your mate. Annie knew from the start she married an imperfect man. (Well, maybe a *nine*, but still imperfect!) And it helps to keep the big picture of all your mate's good qualities in view. The Bible tells us to "think about the good . . . things in others" (Phil. 4:8, TLB), and that's advice to heed if you want to keep irritations in right perspective.

Annie has told you already how our conflict over Christmas celebrations could have led to a major rift between us. But one of the things that helped her accept me when I'd failed miserably to meet her expectations was reminding herself of the big picture. She told me later, "I knew you were acting like a jerk about Christmas. But then I decided, so what? I thought about everything else I know about you—your devotion to the Lord and all you do for your family. And I decided it wasn't worth messing up the wonderful relationship we have the other 364 days a year, just because of Christmas Day."

That same principle is what helps me accept this eternal fussing with the furniture. An occasional stumble over a footstool is a small price to pay for the pleasure of living in a home that's as inviting as she has made ours. And even if her continual rearranging of the nest didn't produce such lovely results, it'd still be a small inconvenience compared to the privilege of sharing life with a woman who shows so much love and grace.

Annie reminds me, too, that if we let them, these irritations can build character, not walls. (Looks to me like she's going to be *quite* a character by the time she's done living with me!) But she has a point.

Remember our definition of romance? It's having a servant's heart, looking for ways to each give to the other out of love for Christ. These irritations can be prime places to give, and sometimes to give in a way that costs us dearly. When we do, we're loving with Christ's love, and He won't let our giving go unrewarded. Sometimes the return He gives comes in the form of changing our mate. Other times, the return is that He changes us to be more patient, or to see the irritation in a different light, or to make it one of the bonding points between us. Some of our funnier moments together now come from some of these irritations that used to drive one or the other of us crazy. For some of our differences, laughter has proved to be the best resolution.

But there's something you need to know. Annie and I *never* make a joke to others about our differences unless it's funny to *both* of us. Jokes about your spouse can easily become thinly veiled attacks, excuses for sarcasm and ridicule. With a quick wit, you can say what you've always wanted to say, then throw up your hands in innocence and claim, "I was only kidding. Why are you always so oversensitive?" There's no quicker way to ruin a romance.

As we've thought about dealing with irritations, we realize we're more fortunate than most. Both Annie and I grew up in homes where our parents provided good examples for us of how to deal with differences. My dad, for instance, never yelled at my mother. Sometimes they whispered intently—very intently—but there was no hollering. I have never heard my parents call each other names, or demean each other, or stomp out of the house in a rage, or strike one another. When differences came up, they were discussed without nagging, or sulking, or whining or threatening. I'm very grateful for such a rich legacy.

But your background may be different, or your mate's may be. Even if that's so, Jesus Christ can become a role model for you as you see the way He spoke the truth in love in Scripture. And you may want to look for Christian couples who can model His ways for you. Dealing with differences requires some skills, and if you don't have them, you can learn them. That's the purpose of resources like the Bill Gothard Seminars, Marriage Encounter, Campus Crusade's Family Life Conferences, or the multitude of other books and tape series you'll find at Christian bookstores. We've found that these teachings have helped us use our irritations as opportunities to grow closer, instead of allowing them to become threats to our love.

But when all the techniques don't work to resolve differences, it will help to remind yourself of the brevity of life. Who knows how long the Lord will give you to be with each other? In light of how quickly our lives speed by, these irritations are, after all, very little.

This Time It's Different

The old man held the hand of his wife
As she lay in the hospital bed.
She was weak and quiet, he had tears in his eyes
As he prayed she would hear what he said.

He said, "Honey, you know it's a mystery to me
How time has made days out of years.
'Cause it seems like yesterday, right down the
    hall,
You and I were here.

"When they cut my finger, honey, you almost
    fainted.
We didn't know gettin' married would hurt.
We were so young and so sincere,
But so sure it would work.
Darlin' we knew it would work.

"Then two years later and two floors down,
Our daughter was born in the fall.
I had to borrow a dime from the doctor—
A proud father must make a call!

"Then some time later we came here again—
I remember our son's broken arm.
You were the one the nurse had to settle.
I had to pay for our car.

"And, honey, it seems like moments ago
We were here when the grandbaby came. . . ."
Then the old man stopped talkin',
And he moved in closer
And begged her to whisper his name.
He prayed she'd just whisper his name.

So many times they had been there together,
And together they always went home.
But this time it's different and the old man cried,
'Cause this time he left there alone.[1]

Let God Handle Your Finances

ANNIE: Before he would perform our wedding, our minister sat Steve and me down to soak up his standard, twelve-minute, premarital pep talk. (Little did we know that twelve *weeks* wouldn't have been enough to prepare us for the leap ahead. Fortunately, we looked at life from a happy mix of youth and ignorance. So we listened, expectantly, to the twelve minutes of advice that would guarantee us fifty or sixty years of romantic bliss.)

Most of what that minister said we heartily "amened." But not everything. "One of the biggest sources of potential problems in your marriage," he told us, "will be *money*." We were too polite to disagree. But when he said that, we knew he couldn't be talking about us, because *we didn't have any money*! How do you have problems with something you don't have? And since our career plans centered around a Christian music ministry, which paid no set income, we didn't figure we'd ever have enough money for it to cause struggles.

We were right about not having money. Our first year

of marriage our gross income came to $3,000. (That *is* gross, isn't it!) But we found to our dismay that no marriage is immune to struggles over the green stuff. We had things to learn *together* about having and not having money. But God started with us individually, teaching each of us that He had to be our provider.

The lessons for me began with my desire for a washer and dryer.

We newly wedded Chapmans had parked ourselves in a garage that had been converted into a tiny two-room apartment. Paying the rent and keeping our old '50 Chevy running ate up most of our meager funds. That's why it seemed absolutely out of the question to talk to Steve about buying a washer and dryer, even though I hated lugging our clothes to the laundromat. I knew that with our income, buying laundry equipment was as possible as buying a Mercedes Benz. Telling Steve about my desire would only hurt him, since there was no way he could provide it for me on his income.

What was a new bride to do? I could wheedle, wail, whine, or work for a washer and dryer. But the thought came to mind that I had a better place to start than any of these. I could pray. God had promised He'd provide all our needs, so I decided to start by asking Him. In the same way a little child would come to her Father, I told God about my desire for a washer and dryer.

And zap! Friends offered us their used set. I was ecstatic when they moved that equipment into our carport. What could be easier than this? Shoot up a little request, and down floats a Maytag, used but still usable!

But before I'd even had a chance to tell Steve about my prayer and its instantaneous answer, my generous husband remembered a couple we knew who'd just had a baby. Surely they needed the washer and dryer more than we did. So he up and gave it to them. I cried to myself while I watched them load *my* washer and dryer onto the truck.

Now what? Maybe I'd missed something in the way I prayed, so I tried it again.

And sure enough, not even a month later, a friend stopped us after church to ask if we needed a new washer and dryer. *New!* No wonder God had allowed the first set to be given away. He had something better for me. I was just drawing a deep breath to shout "hallelujah!" when Steve informed our friend that of course we needed the washer and dryer, but he knew a couple with a new baby who were making do with an old set. Surely they needed it more than we did.

I couldn't believe my ears! Were all the new parents in the world going to have to own laundry equipment before I could be set free from lugging my loads to the laundromat?

When our finances seemed just a bit better, I told Steve how much I wanted laundry equipment, and he agreed it was a need. So we applied for credit and ordered a brand new, beautiful Maytag duo. The night before they were to be delivered, I was so excited I barely slept.

But they never came. Before the delivery truck showed up, the store called to tell us our credit application had been rejected. I was so low I had to look up to see the bottom. The three answers to my prayer had been almost-yes's that slid away into no's. Had I been foolish to pray? Or was I praying wrongly? Could we expect God to get involved in our finances, or not? Not knowing what else to do, I continued to pray for a washer and dryer—and now for patience and understanding as well.

God *did* provide a washer and dryer, and some very interesting side benefits, too.

A few months later, I became pregnant, and with the pregnancy came fainting spells. One day at the laundromat, the heat got to me and I passed out, hitting my head on the concrete floor when I fell. I woke up in the hospital with a concussion, and the doctor told Steve, "This woman is never to do laundry in a laundromat again." So the lady who hated laundromats was medically banished from them forever, leaving Steve to do laundry detail. (And they say there's no justice in the world!)

A few weeks later, Steve learned from a neighbor about a resource that would allow us to buy the exact equipment we'd ordered before, but at *half* the price. So, one night, he took me out to dinner. He'd arranged for his friends to put the new washer and dryer in place while we were gone. When we came home, there they waited, greeting me in all their shiny porcelain glory. There was even a single red rose sitting in a vase on the washer. (Who says laundry can't be romantic?)

A year after I began to pray, God provided beautiful, new laundry equipment. The *way* He chose to work put me through the wringer (sorry about that!), but I came away with lessons I've used again and again in the years since.

First, God wants and is able to provide for us. *Both* Steve and I need to ask Him to help us. Now, He doesn't always provide in the exact way I envision, and He doesn't always act on my timetable. But if He seems slow to work, or says no, it's because He's got a larger and greater good in mind for me.

In our case, because He didn't say yes to me at once, another family was able to enjoy first a used, then a new washer and dryer. Steve and I got the joy of giving generously—twice!—at a time when we didn't have much materially to give. And best of all, perhaps, we were spared of relying on credit as a way to provide our needs. It could have easily become a way of life to look to Mastercard instead of the Master for our provision. Why wait on the

Lord when a three-by-four-inch plastic rectangle could free us from the laundromat right now? Because we couldn't get credit, we had no choice but to wait. And when we waited, God had a chance to work for us and show us He could provide. And He tacked on no interest or carrying charges!

This experience with the washer and dryer helped my faith to grow. And I needed it during the week when, after we paid all our bills, we had only five dollars left over to buy groceries. I can squeeze a nickel till Thomas Jefferson winces, but I knew there was no way I could feed us for a week on five dollars. So I prayed, reminding the Lord He'd promised that His people would not be left to beg for bread. And it came to my mind to ask Him for six invitations to dinner that week. That settled, I went to the store and spent the five dollars on a loaf of bread, a carton of milk, a box of cereal and a pound of bologna—all we needed to cover breakfast and lunch for a week.

And then, though it had never happened before (or since, for that matter), the phone began to ring. To my amazement, we received six calls, each inviting us to dinner for a different night that week.

Another time when we were in need, we walked out on our porch and found a box of groceries there. Still another time money came anonymously in the mail. And there were unexpected opportunities to work for pay. But those early lessons taught me the most important principle I had to learn about money: God is our provider, and a faithful provider He is.

While I was learning the Lessons of the Laundry and the Lunches, God had a financial training program going for Steve as well.

When we first married, our apartment also lacked a refrigerator, so we bought one. And what a refrigerator! For fifteen dollars we came home with one of those round-faced Frigidaires, the kind with enough chrome on it to make it pass for the front end of a Chevy. And though it kept things cool, it had two annoying habits: It walked around the kitchen, and it didn't defrost itself. (Steve discovered this second unfortunate fact the morning he opened the freezer and found it so thoroughly frosted up, he couldn't fit a Popsicle inside.) So in good wifely fashion, I said I'd defrost it.

"Great, sweetheart, great," Steve said. "Just one thing. Don't jab that frozen stuff out with a knife. You may get in a hurry and be tempted; but whatever you do, *don't* go poking into that freezer with anything sharp."

Well, two hours later I was on the phone to my husband. "Steve . . . Honey . . . I was defrosting and (cough, cough) using a knife. And uh, I punctured something, sweetheart. The refrigerator just went *swh-h-h-h-h-h,* and quit." Of course, what I'd done was to puncture the freon tube when I jabbed into it with my knife, and that noise was the life draining from our refrigerator.

Steve said nothing, but I heard a sound like muffled choking noises on the other end of the line. But when Steve came back on, he was the model of Rage Restrained.

"Now, sweetheart," he said evenly, "you know we can't afford another refrigerator, so you'll have to do the best you can." And he told me to take the money we had and get ice and a styrofoam cooler from the Hot Stop down the street. Then he hung up—most likely before he said something he knew he'd regret later.

But even as he was putting down the receiver, a man stuck his head in Steve's door and said, "Do you need a refrigerator? I've got to give one away right now. I've got to catch a flight to Guatemala. My wife and I are going to live there a year, and we've got to get rid of this refrigerator before we go. Do you need one?"

Faster than Richard Petty, Steve zoomed across town

and picked up the refrigerator. It was enormous. It didn't walk around, it had an icemaker, it was self-defrosting *and* it was full of food. Not only did he not have to wait for God to provide, that time he didn't even have to pray.

But seeing such a dramatic provision didn't keep Steve from having his moments of financial panic. Like the time he got a call from his accountant . . . on April 12. And it was the call you never want to get three days before taxes are due.

"I hate to break the news to you," the man began, "but you owe some extra money this year."

"How much?" Steve asked.

And after Steve got back up off the floor, he told the man, "We don't have that kind of money."

"Do the best you can," the accountant said. "You've got three days."

I'd like to report that Steve responded with a jubilant cry of faith, but that wasn't so. He crawled off to the bedroom and slumped on the edge of the bed. He told me later he sat there wondering what it was going to be like in jail. But in his moment of desperation, words starting coming to him. The result was the song you'll find at the end of this chapter, called "Things Are Lookin' Right for a Miracle."

It was a message only desperate ears could have heard. And a miracle was ahead. That afternoon Steve got an invitation to sing in place of another person who'd taken ill. He got back from the concert the night of April 14, and wrote out a check for the taxes.

Maybe you're starting to think we believe it's important to trust God for your finances. And you're right! Perhaps we believe it so strongly because we're not very sophisticated in financial matters and we know we need all the help we can get. Or maybe we believe it because the Bible says that's how God intends things to work. He never planned we'd have to worry and stew over money. Jesus said our Father wants to care for us as completely as He does the sparrows and the lilies so we can be free to love Him and to enjoy the life He created for us.

Of course, one of the ways we stop Him from caring for our finances is by refusing to wait for Him to do things His way.

The Need for "Wait" Training

"Wait" is a four-letter word. And in our age, that's especially true when it comes to material things. It's easy to look at all that stuff our parents have crammed in the attic, the garage and the storage building down the road and think we're failures if we haven't acquired in two years of marriage what it took them twenty or thirty years to pile up.

The push to have it all *now* creates at least two pitfalls that are easy for any couple to fall into.

They may fall prey to what Steve calls the "Shop-Like-a-Bull Syndrome" (in other words, *charge everything!*). When we didn't have money for a washer and dryer, what did we think of? Buy now—pay later, of course. But charging and chocolate have something in common. Just a taste makes you crazy for more . . . and more . . . and *more*.

A friend of ours loves to tell of the time his American Express card was stolen, but he refused to try to find it because the thief was using it less than his wife did! Because of the entrapment inherent in credit, Steve and I decided to pay cash as we go, not using credit cards unless we know we can pay them off at the end of the month. And if, in case of a real emergency, we couldn't follow through on our end-of-the-month commitment, we agreed together not to charge again until the balance we owe reads zero. We're not only protecting ourselves from living beyond our means, but we've saved a bundle in interest and carrying charges.

And limiting our use of credit forces us to wait on God so He gets a chance to provide for us His way.

Another financial pitfall eager to engulf couples is the "Double-Your-Income, Double-Your-Fun" snare. When both husband and wife earn a paycheck, it's tempting to base their lifestyle on the assumption that both incomes will always be available. But life can quickly prove us wrong. One spouse loses his job, or illness hits, or a pregnancy comes as a surprise. The result? Increased expenses, yet only half the income to meet them.

We don't have two independent incomes, but if you do, we'd encourage you to consider budgeting your necessities (mortgage payment, groceries, and the like) on just one of your salaries. The second paycheck could then be used to save for a house, or investments, or wants not quite as essential as food and shelter.

We've always had a savings account. Even that first year together we managed to save $200. No matter how small the savings may be, we've made ourselves put something away.

And we've always given at least 10 percent of our income to God's work. Whether the checks we receive are $100 or $10,000, we take God's share out first because we want to, and because we believe keeping God's share for ourselves only makes us vulnerable to attacks of the devil.

God wants us to serve Him, not money. Richard Foster, in his penetrating book *Money, Sex, and Power*, has challenged us to never succumb to letting money determine our decisions. He says:

> The Christian is given the high calling of *using* mammon [money] without serving mammon. We are using mammon when we allow God to deter-

mine our economic decisions. We are serving mammon when we allow mammon to determine our economic decisions. We simply must decide who is going to make our decisions—God or mammon.

Do we buy a particular home on the basis of the call of God, or because of the availability of money? Do we buy a new car because we can afford it, or because God instructed us to buy a new car? If money determines what we do or don't do, then money is our boss. If God determines what we do or don't do, then God is our boss. My money might say to me, "You have enough to buy that," but my God might say to me, "I don't want you to have it." Now, whom am I to obey?[1]

Making It Through the Money Maze

So far, I've told you a lot about what Steve and I learned individually about money, and I've let you in on some things we agree about. But it's not always financial bliss under the Chapman roof. Our premarital warning about money being a sure source of tension for a couple wasn't wrong. And money—how we get it and what we do with it—has caused tension for us from time to time.

I grew up in a little community where everyone knew everyone else's business. So my dad, to save himself some embarrassment, arranged with our banker to cover any outstanding checks his kids wrote. Therefore, keeping a balanced checkbook was never a burning need for me because I always knew Daddy would make up any deficits. This worked well—that is, until I married. Steve made it clear he was my husband, not my father, and that I'd henceforth need to take responsibility for recording the

[1]Richard Foster, *Money, Sex and Power* (New York: Harper and Row, 1985), 56.

amounts of money I parted with.

On the whole, I've done quite well at keeping my accounts in order. But not long ago, I let things slide and we got a call from the bank. When my husband came home from paying out forty-five dollars in overdraft charges, he was in a foul mood, to say the least. In the tirade that followed, I found out once again how amazingly articulate Steve can be, and how completely he's able to vent his feelings.

The problem was, he was dead right. And when he finished laying out his case, he leaned over and peered at me and said, "Will this *ever* happen again?"

I looked back with the same seriousness. "Yes, it will," I told him, "but not for a long, long time."

Who can stay mad at such an honest woman?

Our money differences don't always end so easily, but we need to remember that finances is one area of life where couples desperately need to learn to talk together, laugh together, and keep on growing together. We live in a culture that worships things, a society where people find it easier to share their bodies than they do their bank accounts. A long time ago, I heard someone say, "We spend money we don't have, to buy things we don't need, to impress people we don't like." Surely this isn't what God intended.

Money is a resource, a tool for us to use together in His service. It was intended to be our slave, not to enslave us. The stewardship of it was intended to draw us together, not to push us apart.

If money squabbles are pushing you apart, it's only wise to seek help. Maybe the two of you did well together during the early years when you had fewer things, but now with increased income has come increased conflict. Today, Steve and I more often find ourselves on the giving end than the receiving end, and we've discovered it in-

volves responsibilities and decisions we didn't have to face
as newlyweds. We've been greatly helped by attending
Christian money management seminars, and then talking
together about which of the principles will work for us.
(You might enjoy reading together some of the books suggested at the end of this chapter, and using them as a
springboard for discussing your money differences.)

Though we didn't know it all those years ago, our pastor was right. Money *can* be a major source of conflict in
marriage. But we know now, too, it can also be an arena
for learning lessons of faith that will make us closer than
ever. They can even provide the space God needs to do a
miracle!

Things Are Looking Right for a Miracle

Well, the money's getting tight,
And we're working day and night,
But, we can't seem to fit the ends together.
And way down in our souls
The wind of fear is a-blowin',
And I know it's bringin' in some stormy weather.

But before it gets to you,
There is something you can do
That will help you when you're facing your
      recession.
In your heart get on your knees,
Be like Moses at the seas,
And let God hear you make this good confession:

Things are looking right for a miracle!
Ain't no reason I should get hysterical.
Open up the doors,
God, you've done it before.
Things are looking right for a miracle.

Now, it may not be your money,
But some other kind of pain.
Let God get the glory, your confession is the
    same:

Things are looking right for a miracle!
Ain't no reason I should get hysterical.
Open up the doors,
God, you've done it before.
Things are looking right for a miracle![2]

Suggested Readings on Financial Planning

1. Richard Foster, *Money, Sex and Power* (Harper and Row, 1985).
2. Ron Blue, *Master Your Money: A Step-by-Step Plan for Financial Freedom* (Thomas Nelson, 1986).
3. Larry Burkett, *The Complete Financial Guide for Young Couples* (Moody, 1989).
4. Wm. Brock Thoene, *Protecting Your Income and Your Family's Future* (Bethany House Publishers, 1989).

---

[2]"Things Are Looking Right for a Miracle." Lyrics by Steve Chapman. © Copyright 1981 by Dawn Treader Music (SEASAC) and Snowfox Music (SESAC). All rights reserved. International copyright secured. Used by permission of Gaither Copyright Management.

Staying in Like

ANNIE: People get married because they love each other. But I believe they stay married because they *like* each other. And because I believe this, I'm a great crusader for falling in like, and staying in like with your spouse.

My penchant to promote "like" in marriage may never result in songs that make the Top 20, simply because it's so difficult to rhyme. Look at love. You can pair it up with sticky sentiments like "my turtle dove" and "the stars above." Unfortunately, "like" rhymes only with expressions like "take a hike." Hardly the sentiments passionate ballads are made of.

But *liking* has a wonderful thing going for it: Partners who like each other have a relationship founded on respect—respect for their mate and for themselves as well. When respect, and the "liking" it fosters, flourishes in a marriage, you can bet the relationship rests on very solid ground.

So how can you put more like in your marriage? We've found five things that work for us.

First, don't try to be everything to each other.

Steve is my closest friend, but he isn't my only friend. For instance, there's Nancy, the one I can complain to on those days I feel like an absolute failure as a parent. She understands what I'm feeling in a way that Steve doesn't, simply because he isn't a mom. (One parenting authority has said that though both parents can love their offspring, mothers are "anchored differently" in their children, and I agree.)

Because Nancy is gracious enough to let me unload, she's spared Steve from having to endure numerous bouts of moaning and self-recrimination on my part when I get down about my parental shortcomings. Now, Nancy and I give each other more than just a shoulder to cry on when one of us isn't the mom she should be. But her friendship to me meets needs that probably wouldn't be met in the same way if she weren't part of my life.

Steve has friends like this, too. Because Wendall is his golfing buddy, he has enjoyable companionship that he'd never get from me on the golf course. (For me, mixing greens and a good time can only mean going out to a salad bar for lunch!)

God intended that our relationship take priority over others, but He never intended that we exclaim, "Us two will do!" We're part of an enormous family of brothers and sisters in the faith. They need us, and we need them. We believe these relationships with others *enhance* our liking for each other. They add a dimension to us personally we couldn't get if our circle of two never expanded to include anyone else. As we grow *individually*, our life together grows, too, because we have more to bring to our marriage.

Second, give each other time alone.

Yes, these words do come from a woman who traded her picket fence for months in a motor home just so she could be next to the man she loved. You surely have no doubts by now of how imperative we believe it is that couples be together. But it's also important that you give each other time alone.

Steve requires occasional bouts of solitary-ness to recharge his emotional batteries. It's easy to spot when he's been around people (even me) too much, because his creativity dries up. So he needs time to tromp through the woods, or head out for a deserted golf course. Or when he's ready to write music, he holes up in a motel for a few days.

Me, I just need time when no one will ask me for a decision, but I don't have to be absolutely alone. That's why I can take off for an afternoon in a shopping mall and come back refreshed. (I was going to say I came back "all charged up.")

Some of our time alone we each devote to reading God's Word and to prayer. Though Steve and I are deeply bonded in Christ, God still sees and relates to each of us individually. And He holds us accountable individually for how we obey and love Him. I am Steve's wife, yet more importantly, I'm God's daughter. He speaks to me; He hears my prayers; He works with me, sometimes in the same way He works with Steve, but sometimes in a very different way.

Giving ourselves to God requires that each of us spend time alone with Him, reading His Word and sharing ourselves with Him in prayer. Giving each other time to develop this personal intimacy with God is what helps set our love free. Our marriage matters terribly to us, but it can't be the center of our lives. Only Jesus Christ is worthy of that honor. If we don't each develop our relationship with Him, we may be in danger of worshiping His gift of marriage instead of worshiping the Giver, Christ. This was the sin Paul warned about in Romans 1, and those committing it were headed for destruction.

Jesus Christ is the glue that holds our marriage together. Colossians 1:17 says, "In him all things hold together." Without the bonding He provides, we wouldn't have a marriage worth preserving.

Third, if you want a marriage of long-term like, be likable.

Do you and your spouse tell each other *everything*? We don't. For instance, Steve does not know how much I weigh. And I've never pressed for details about the women in his life before I came along.

Please don't get me wrong. We don't advocate purposely withholding information from each other as a manipulative tool to get your own way. But telling each other every thought and every detail of every life transaction can lead to boredom, and destroy the mystery and allure that drew you to each other at the start. In short, it can make it harder for you to like each other.

I remember hearing about the husband who complained, "I work in a pressure-cooker atmosphere all day, and so when I come home, it's difficult to respond enthusiastically when I'm greeted with an eighteen-minute account of our baby's attempts to learn to go poo-poo by herself."

This husband needed to appreciate that his wife worked in a pressure-cooker of her own. But it also behooves his wife to remember how much of her man's daily conversation takes place with people who talk about things for which he naturally has great passion. And if she's to continue to retain his respect, she'd be wise to balance the perils of potty-training with conversation he finds more intellectually stimulating. And he needs to do the same for her.

After all, when you choose a friend, don't you look for someone who's pleasant, attractive and enjoyable to be with? I don't tend to stay in long-term friendships with people who are always negative, or boring, or unhappy, and I shouldn't expect Steve to, either. Because he's committed to Christ and he loves me, I believe he'll never abandon me. But I want that "staying" to be as fun for him as possible. I don't want to just be his wife; I want to be someone he'd choose as a good friend, even if we weren't married. In short, I want to be someone he likes.

And he likes me as I like him. Three easy actions help me dwell on Steve's good qualities, and they may help you as well.

Talk to your spouse about his or her strengths. Others can tell me I've sung well, but when Steve says it, well . . . it means so much more.

Thank your spouse for the big things and the little things he or she does for you. We can so easily take for granted the ways our mate serves us. Have you thanked your husband recently for how hard he works? Have you told your wife how much you appreciate the kindnesses she shows to your parents?

Surprise your mate with acts of service he or she doesn't expect. It may be making your special peach cobbler on a night when no guests are coming, or choosing to rent a video you know she'd love, though you'd rather watch Monday Night Football.

Fourth, grow in respect for yourself.

I love the furniture available at discount stores, that cheap, fake-wood-grain-over-plywood stuff. Yes, I know that in probably a year and a half it will have all fallen apart and we'll be using it for kindling, but that doesn't deter me a bit.

Now that I think about it, I may not be the best judge of whether or not a piece of furniture is cheap. I remember the time Steve and I picked up the cutest little walnut wall decoration at a garage sale for less than two dollars. A real buy, we thought. So we carted it home and nailed it up with a plant and a couple of other do-dads next to it on the wall.

Well, we both stood there gloating over how great it looked. In fact, we decided, it looked a little too great. That walnut had such depth and gloss, it made the other furniture in the room look awful. Somehow we hadn't noticed before how marred and tacky our stuff really was because there'd been nothing to compare it to. As the days went by, that furniture seemed to look worse and worse, until we finally gave in and got some new pieces.

Ah-h-h-h! Now our wall grouping was surrounded by furniture worthy of it. But boy, did that new furniture ever make the carpet look shabby! So it wasn't long before—up came the rug and down went some plush carpeting, rich enough to do justice to the furniture. But the carpet looked so good it made the walls practically scream for a new coat of paint, and who were we to turn a deaf ear to screeching walls?

That paint job did for the room all we hoped it would. The place couldn't have looked better. And as long as we stayed in the room, we were 100 percent content. But, of course the moment we went anywhere else in the house, we became sickeningly aware of how awful everything else looked. So, quicker than you could send off for a subscription to *Better Homes and Gardens*, we started sprucing up the rest of the house. And $24,000 later, we ended up with a house worthy of that $2 wall decoration.

(Both of us have sworn off garage sales forever. We decided we simply can't afford them!)

But back to the discount house furniture. One day, I found the most wonderful bookcase on sale. It was a huge thing, with doors and drawers—the works! And the price was so ridiculously low I couldn't resist. For that price it came disassembled, of course, but they assured me that a child could put it together.

The "child" they had in mind must have been a nine-teen-year-old mechanical genius with an engineering degree from M.I.T. At least that's what I concluded when I hauled the thing in the house and settled into the living room to put it together. I knew I was in trouble when it took me half an hour just to open the box. (This box must have been designed by the same sadist who created those permanently sealed bags the honey-roasted peanuts on airplanes come in. I finally took a butcher knife and sawed the box open. You'll not find this use for butcher knives recommended by your home economists, but I figured it was better than using the knife to attack the box designer.)

Unfortunately, I was soon to discover that opening the box was the *easy* part. Inside I found 436 fake-veneer pieces that all looked exactly alike, and a set of instructions that might just as well have been written in Japanese. There were lots of directives about gluing Part A to Part L, but neither A nor L were marked.

Struggling to make sense of this pile of wood was challenge enough for a woman whose former construction experience had been limited to Lego block towers and gingerbread houses. But I had the added pressure of a skeptical supervisor. You see, when I hauled this box into the house, Steve naturally assumed he would have to put the bookcase together. Since he knew he'd enjoy this task about as much as he would having a root canal without novocaine, he rolled his eyes and let me know in no uncertain terms that assembling a bookcase was not his idea of a fun way to spend the evening. He had other plans.

"I know that," I responded brightly. "I'm planning to put it together myself."

My husband's face formed itself into a disbelieving smirk.

That was all I needed, so I ripped open (or, more accurately, sawed into) that box and determined that from this pile of paper boards a bookcase would arise.

Well, I succeeded—with a little help from Heidi. And the bookcase looked so great I ran right out and bought two more!

Something more significant than furniture came from all that lumber-locking. I'd faced a new challenge and met it, and I liked myself more for having done so.

Respecting yourself is an important component to a happy marriage. And I've found that my self-respect grows most quickly when I'm stretching and growing and venturing into new challenges. For you, bookcases may be no challenge. Maybe you need to take up a sport you've always feared, or install the garage-door opener yourself, or stay alone with the baby for an entire weekend while your wife takes off to a women's conference. When you're taking new territory, you no longer need to demand that your mate be your only source of self-respect. And your growing confidence can make you a more attractive marriage partner.

But there is an epilogue to my bookcase venture that might be helpful as a caution. By the time I got well along with the second bookcase, Steve spent more and more time hanging around, watching me.

"I'm doing just great," I assured him.

I expected he'd be relieved and head back to his own projects. But he didn't.

"I suppose I could finish this up for you," he offered.

"No thanks," I assured him breezily. "I know what I'm doing now."

"But I could do it faster," he countered.

His insistence finally caught my attention. Here I was, delivering him from giving up an evening doing something he really didn't enjoy, and he was fussing with me for a chance to help. What was happening?

"Steve," I finally asked him, "do you feel funny with me doing this by myself, like I don't need you?"

"I guess it does make me feel kind of funny," he admitted.

So I suggested we do the next one together. This proved to sound better than it was. When I hammer, it's *tap, tap, tap.* But when Steve hammers, it's *ka-poweey!* So I nearly got my finger broken when I held a nail in place for him. This, perhaps, is why you never see highway billboards promising that the family who hammers together stays together!

But Steve's response brings up an important caution. Any time either marriage partner makes a change (even a change for the better), it brings about a change in the balance of the marriage. And change can be threatening, or at least uncomfortable, just because it's different. Though Steve was proud of my new skill, it also didn't feel quite right to him, simply because I was poking into an area that had previously been his domain. Now, his feelings were short-lived and easy to put into perspective. It didn't take long to realize that an evening or two sticking furniture together didn't mean I'd be abandoning him in order to accept the presidency of Carpenters' Local 301.

But in the delicate dynamic that makes up marriage, change and growth can make our partners feel unsure; so as we take on new challenges, we need to surround those we love with the reassurance they need to see that we're growing together.

Fifth, your respect will grow as you continue to share your hearts.

How easy it is to get so busy in the logistics of keeping life going that we fail to share our deepest hearts with each other. That's why I so often come home from a singing trip with my family and tell Steve, "We really need to get some time together!" This sounds like a paradox, I know, since we've just spend seventy-two hours inches away from each other in a van or airplane seats, or quarters almost as close. But it isn't. What we have on those trips is physical and work time together; but in the responsibilities of work and family, we don't always have opportunity for the kind of soul exchange that keeps our hearts beating as one.

For that kind of time, we usually have to get away. That often means a "date"—out to dinner, or maybe even to a motel for the night. And in these times, we have some ground rules. We don't go to movies, because we're not together to hear someone else talk . . . we need to hear *each other.* And we don't talk about the kids. Or about work decisions. We try to focus solely on each other.

Sometimes gimmicks can be a help in opening up to each other. One marriage counselor has couples each write down: (1) The three things I like best about our marriage. (2) The one thing I'd most like to see changed in our marriage.

You can imagine that the answer to these questions could give a couple an interesting evening together.

We've also enjoyed communication quizzes. I'm including a dozen questions to draw from if you need help sharing your hearts with each other. We've found that talking about questions like these together helps us look at parts of our life in new light.

1. What first attracted you to your spouse?
2. What characteristic do you most admire about your mate?
3. Name two things your spouse has done for you that you would consider romantic.
4. Name one thing your spouse likes you to do for him/her.
5. What changes would you like to make in the way you relate to your spouse?
6. What changes would you like to see your spouse make in your relationship as a couple?
7. How has your parents' relationship influenced how you get along with your spouse?
8. List your spouse's greatest needs.
9. List your greatest needs.
10. If you had the power to change one thing about yourself, what would it be?
11. If you had the power to change one thing about your spouse, what would it be?
12. What do you both most need to change in order to keep your relationship top priority in your lives?

Goal-Setting

On a regular basis (every three or six months, or year), we go away with a specific intent to set and review goals for our life together. We cover the three areas that matter most to us: the family, our individual growth, and our ministry.

Management experts would probably shake their heads in disbelief when they see the simple approach we take to this goal-setting business. Every time I start to list personal goals, losing weight goes down as number one . . . again. And Steve always writes down some version of his desire to become a more vibrant spiritual leader.

Family goals always seem to start out with us determining to take another crack at having regular, meaningful family devotions. (We've done much better the last couple of years, but this one is such a struggle for us, we never seem to be able to take it for granted.) Our family list usually includes something about moving toward getting out of debt, or sticking more closely to the budget.

We do come up with new goals, too, but I'm telling you about our staples so you know your goals don't have to impress Lee Iacocca—they just have to be useful for you.

We set ministry goals for the year to come, then for five years, and for the years until retirement.

The Bible wisely asks, "Can two walk together except they be agreed?" (Amos 3:3). We've found these times of talking about our goals do help keep us in agreement about where we're headed. And they've also given us a chance to look back at where we've been. A wise person once said that a history together prepares people for their future. Reviewing our past has reminded us of how much we have invested in our life together and helps us deepen our determination to make that investment pay off.

Of course, it's not always this serious. Sometimes our times together are mostly just laughing, or sharing our love, or simply being together. That's the beauty of being married. The world does not have to shake every time the two of you are alone. Sometimes the quietness of being together can feed the soul with the knowledge of your oneness.

Real love lives in the heart-openness the two of you share. True love starts with a "kiss of hearts," and falling in *like* is the way to make that kiss happen.

I remember when I met you,
We became good friends.

We started growin' close like a sister and brother.
Then the hand of God stirred our hearts
And brought us closer still,
Though our lips had never met, we knew
We were right for one another.

'Cause true love starts with a kiss of hearts.
It's a touch within
That makes it all begin.
If we're lookin' for love in mere affection,
We're lookin' in the wrong direction,
'Cause true love starts
With a kiss of hearts.

Most of us wanna be in love,
And given time we will.
The sun can shine on us all in due season.
It can lead a couple down the aisle
To pledge their love and lives,
And a kiss may be the end result
But it should never be the reason.

That God alone would lead us into lovin' is my
    prayer.
And when He does I know that He will keep us
    well aware
That true love starts with a kiss of hearts.[1]

---

[1]"Kiss of Hearts." Lyrics by Mickey Cates. © Copyright 1984 by StraightWay Music
(ASCAP). All rights reserved. International copyright secured. Used by permission
of Gaither Copyright Management.

Filling Up Your Cup of Love

STEVE: I've never been one to put much stock in dreams. Give me a pepperoni pizza about 10:30 at night, and I can dream the weirdest stuff, like hairpins chasing me around the room, and even worse. Because that's true, I assume most of my dreams contain more messages from my digestive system than messages from the Lord.

But occasionally my dreams stop me short, and their message is so clear, so appropriate I know it's God, and not a gastronomical vision.

Such was the case when Annie and I were dating. During those days I drove a big old '50 Chevy we named Sarah (Sarah, because like Abraham's wife, she was still productive in her old age). But back to my dream . . .

I was driving down the interstate in Sarah, with Annie sitting close beside me. The day was cold—icy cold—so Annie reached through the steering wheel to turn up the heat. But the steering wheel was loaded with chrome, and the big buttons on Annie's coat sleeve got twisted in the steering wheel, and as she tugged to get free, she jerked the wheel and the car veered to the left and down an embankment.

We careened off the road, and toward a huge open field. But the field was surrounded by a large chain-link fence topped with barbed wire. To the fence was attached a large, official-looking sign that warned, NO TRESPASSING! But we plowed right through the fence, and came to a stop. Suddenly, everything was silent, and I thought, "What happened?"

I looked up, and ahead I saw a beautiful home, shining on the hill, with a concrete drive leading up to it. Then a voice said to me, "That is where I was taking you, but because you trespassed, you will not make it there." Suddenly I heard sirens wailing, and government officials came to drag Annie and me off in opposite directions so we could never be together again. . . .

Whew!

It didn't take two sessions with a shrink to figure out the clear warning of this dream. Annie and I were growing to love each other, and as a result our feelings were "heating up." And the Lord intended that we make a beautiful life together (thus the *Better Homes and Gardens* house I saw on the hill). But there was only one way to that home: the road of purity. If we gave in to sexual involvement before our marriage, we'd be trespassers, crashing through the boundary of marriage God set around sexual union, and we'd miss ever knowing the real oneness He intended for us to enjoy.

It was a warning we needed, because like most young couples we were beginning to encounter moments when our hormones shouted so loudly it was nearly impossible to remember all those Bible verses about temptation we'd learned so diligently. Sexual desire can have such a massive pull that without God's help, we can let it take us places we never intended to go.

Do you know the Bible account of Amnon and Tamar, found in 2 Samuel 13? It's a true story of passion out of control, and illustrates well the terrible price we may have to pay for moments of sexual pleasure outside of marriage.

Amnon was "in luv." He was sure of it. He was so smitten by his desire for the beautiful Tamar that Scripture says he "became frustrated to the point of illness." Now, that's deep feeling! Sexual desire can be just that overwhelming. It can make rational human beings act like total morons; and if we underestimate its power, we're as foolish as the man who throws a lighted match into a barrel of gasoline and expects nothing to happen.

On the other hand, sexual desire can generate positive energy also. Scripture says that when a man and woman join themselves physically, a mysterious spiritual, emotional and psychological bonding happens. God intended that the one we'd give ourselves to would merge with us. The uniqueness and the beauty of a shared sexual experience was designed to be a powerful part of the glue that melds man and wife together for all of life. And the power to create new life rests in the miracle of sexual union.

So sex is like nuclear power—it can explode or it can be channeled. When it is directed toward God's purposes, it can generate the heat we need to love as we should, to serve as He intended, and to create as He planned. As Dr. Richard Dobbins, director of a mental health treatment center in Akron, Ohio, explains:

> [The] primary purpose [of sex] is to enable a husband and wife to build a bond of love between them that will be strong enough to manage the stress of bearing children, raising them, launching them into lives of their own and supporting each other until death parts them.[1]

---

[1]Richard D. Dobbins, Ph.D., "Helping Teens Wait Until Marriage," *Ministries Today* (March/April 1987), 37.

But used wrongfully, havoc and hurt every bit as total can result.

That's what happened with Amnon. The woman for whom he longed was off limits because she was his step-sister. So we have the lovesick Amnon and the out-of-reach Tamar. Onto the scene steps Amnon's friend Jon-adab, with an idea to get around God's restrictions. "What you need," Jonadab advised, "is just a chance to be alone with this girl, to let her know how you feel. Pretend you're sick," he told Amnon. "When King David comes to see you, tell him you'll only recover after you've had a little of that special bread Tamar bakes so well. Ask him to send Tamar to you."

So Amnon deceived his father as his friend suggested, and manipulated the meeting with Tamar. After Tamar baked her special recipe and brought the bread to Amnon, he refused to eat. He ordered everyone from the room, then invited Tamar into his bedroom, "so I may eat from your hand," he told her. (How's that for a weak line?)

When Tamar followed him into his bedroom, he made it clear it was the baker he wanted, not the bread. "Come to bed with me, my sister," he demanded.

Tamar resisted. She reminded him of the wickedness of immorality. Then she appealed to his feeling for her. "What about me?" she pleaded. "Where could I get rid of my disgrace?" And she appealed to his pride. "And what about you? You would be like one of the wicked fools in Israel." But none of these arguments could overcome Am-non's passion, and he raped Tamar.

One thing Amnon's action makes clear: A big sin is usually preceded by a lot of little sins. I doubt that back when Amnon was first attracted to Tamar the idea of rape entered his mind. But he said yes to the sin of lying to his father; then he gave in to the sin of lying to Tamar; then agreed mentally to the sin of immorality. He didn't simply leap off a cliff from purity to sin; he descended there one compromise at a time.

But the most interesting part of this story to me is what follows. Remember that we're dealing with a man who loved this woman so desperately and completely that he became physically sick with desire for her. Now his fantasy is fulfilled: He's joined with her sexually. What response would you expect from him? Wouldn't you think his love for her would burst into full bloom?

Listen to what happened.

"Then [after the rape] Amnon hated her with intense hatred. In fact, he hated her more than he had loved her. Amnon said to her, 'Get up and get out.' " And when she refused to leave, he called his servant and had her thrown out. (See 2 Samuel 13:15-17.) Sexual consummation out of God's plan won't eliminate the tension in a relationship; it only creates more. Sin never unites; it always divides.

Counselor Roger Hillerstrom says, "Every couple coming to me for counseling who have had premarital sexual relations have had postmarital sexual adjustment problems." And he told of a young Christian woman who sat in his office telling a story he hears all too frequently.

> I don't know what happened to our relationship. When Tom and I were dating, we felt so good about each other. We had everything going for us, and we seemed to communicate so well. We did go a bit farther physically than we had planned, but it all seemed so right. Now we haven't even reached our first anniversary, and we feel like strangers. We don't understand each other emotionally—and sexually, there's nothing there. It's become a duty that I perform for him, and he doesn't seem to think that it's very special either. How on earth could two people change so much so quickly?

Because he's heard this story so often, when a couple comes to him for premarital counseling, Hillerstrom asks them to agree to refrain from sexual intercourse until their wedding night. If they refuse, he tells them there's no way they can realistically prepare for marriage, and he gives them three reasons why.

First, God forbids sexual union outside of marriage. When a couple chooses to ignore Him, they're starting their life together in a pattern of disobedience, so He won't be able to help them establish the closeness for which they long. And a clear conscience between them and God is destroyed.

Second, focusing your relationship on sex may keep you from ever finding true intimacy.

We call sex "intimate," but that ain't necessarily so. Real intimacy is a deep and total sharing of your inner self—your joys and woes and hopes and griefs—with another. Hillerstrom says, "To be intimate with a person is to be open, vulnerable, emotionally exposed and trusting. But sexual intercourse can occur without any of that!" It's possible to have sex with a total stranger and to feel, for a moment, a surge somewhat akin to intimacy that isn't real intimacy at all.

The truth is, if there's tension in a couples' relationship, it's possible for them to *avoid* working it out by simply hopping into bed. They leave feeling great about each other for a little while, but the real issues between them have only been covered up, not healed, and in time these festering sores will erupt into gaping, ugly wounds.

Third, when a couple is sexually involved before marriage, they prepare themselves to feel sexual satisfaction only in illicit situations. It's like this. Something deep inside each person engaged in premarital sex says, "We shouldn't be doing this." And that's what makes it exciting. There is something definitely stimulating in the wrongness of the act. That illicitness is part of what brings sexual arousal prior to the marriage, and the couple are conditioning themselves to require it. But after the wedding—*poof!* What was once illegal is now perfectly legal, even expected. When it's not wrong, then it's no longer fun.

So how do these two find sexual excitement? With an affair, of course. Bingo! Great sex again, but only so long as it remains illicit. What a trap to be caught in![2]

We could add a couple of other problems that we've seen emerge from premarital involvement. For one thing, it opens the door to the *destruction of trust*. One couple who had lived together for several months before their marriage finally divorced over this issue of trust. The wife said, "I remember how easy it was to get him into bed with me, and I can't get it out of my mind that another woman could get him just as easily as I did." She probably has a point. If a man and woman don't respect the marriage commitment enough to honor its boundaries before they marry, what's to guarantee they'll suddenly change just because they've walked down the aisle of a church?

Real love can *wait*, but lust has to have what it wants *right now*. So couples involved outside of marriage have begun their life together on a basis of lust, not love. Lust isn't a force strong enough to keep a couple together for life. And marriage isn't a cure for lust. It is only the ground wherein seeds of *disrespect* are able to root and grow between them.

Perhaps as you've read this you're thinking back to your own courtship. If you were involved sexually before your marriage, you may be feeling great guilt or despair as you understand the gravity of what you've done.

If that's true, I come to you with words of hope. God

---

[2]P. Roger Hillerstrom, "The Eroding Effects of Premarital Sex," *The Standard* (December 1984), 13–16.

convicts us of our sin only in order that He might cleanse and heal us. And the God we serve is not only Creator; He is the Re-Creator. He can take your marriage and cleanse it, and bring it to a state of purity before Him so that you can live your lives together on a solid foundation.

When Annie and I talk with couples who've sinned in premarital sex, we have them take each other's hand and pray like this:

> *Father, we admit our wrongdoing. We have sinned against you and each other. Please forgive us. Cleanse us from our wrong and the guilt we rightly feel. In your mercy, help us begin anew right now, starting life together on the strong foundation of purity. We commit ourselves to each other completely and exclusively for the rest of our lives, and we look to you for the grace to keep this commitment until death parts us. Amen.*

When you ask Him to forgive you, He promises He will (1 John 1:9). And He also promises to make you as pure before Him as if you'd never sinned in the first place (Isa. 1:18).

Past Involvements Before Marriage

About six months after we were married, Annie ran into a friend who'd also married about the time we did. When Annie asked how their life together was going, the woman admitted she was bored. Married only six months, and bored *already*? The woman went on to explain that she had been involved with a number of other men before she married Tom, and now her husband hadn't turned out to be quite as sexually exciting as some of the others.

It's now fourteen years later, and this couple has survived their rocky beginning and have gone on to serve Christ. But they made it only by going through a bout of confession and experiencing God's cleansing of the past.

Sexuality, you see, is a lot like adhesive tape. It's not made to be used over and over. The strongest bond adhesive tape can form is with the first surface it sticks to. Of course, you can pull off a piece of tape and reapply it to other surfaces a number of times and it will still stick. But every time you do, it loses some of its ability to bond until it finally won't stick to anything.

Richard Dobbins (to whom I'm indebted for this adhesive tape idea) explains it this way: "Sexuality and bonding are inseparable. We cannot express ourselves sexually without affecting the bonding ability of our bodies."[3]

Sexual liaisons with anyone other than your spouse can only have bad effects. Even if the experience was good, it creates the problem Annie's friend had: longing for someone other than her mate. If the experience was bad, it can leave you with negative feelings about sex that may then be targeted at your marriage partner.

But again, there can be cleansing and healing when we come to Christ and admit our wrong. After David had sinned with Bathsheba, he came to God with this prayer:

> Have mercy on me, O God, according to your unfailing love; according to your great compassion blot out my transgressions. Wash away all my iniquity and cleanse me from my sin. (Psalm 51:1–2, NIV)

I'm not recommending that you sit down with your mate and rehearse the details of any pre- or extra-marital encounters with others. Access to this kind of information only gives Satan all kinds of weapons with which to torment your mate with fears, doubts and bitterness. If you've confessed to the Lord and still don't feel forgiven,

---

[3]Richard D. Dobbins, Ph.D., "Helping Teens Wait Until Marriage," *Ministries Today* (March/April 1987), 37–42.

you may want to make confession to a trusted Christian friend, or spiritual advisor. Allow them to hear your confession, and assure you of Christ's cleansing. Then go forth as David did, expecting to experience the joy of unhindered fellowship with the Lord, and give yourself freely and fully in love to your mate.

Married, but Not Dead

Just because you've made a sexual commitment to your spouse doesn't necessarily follow that you'll never feel a twinge of attraction to anyone else. In these times when sexual temptations seem to have saturated our world, we've established some guidelines to help us stay true to the Lord and to each other.

In an article in *Moody Monthly*, Jerry Jenkins, vice president for publishing of Moody Press, set down his personal rules for, as he calls it, putting a hedge around his marriage. We found his list read just as ours would. Mr. Jenkins says this:

1. Whenever I need to meet, or dine, or travel with an unrelated woman, I make it a threesome. Should an unavoidable last-minute complication make this impossible, my wife hears it from me first.
2. I am careful about touching. While I might shake hands or squeeze an arm or shoulder in greeting, I embrace only dear friends or relatives, and only in front of others.
3. If I pay a compliment, it is on clothes or hairstyle, not on the person herself. Commenting on a pretty outfit is much different, in my opinion, than telling a woman that she herself looks pretty.
4. I avoid flirtation or suggestive conversation, even in jest.

Jenkins goes on to say, "These rules will appear prudish

because my mentioning them when necessary has elicited squints, scowls and not-so-hidden smiles of condescension."[4] We've sometimes met with the same reaction.

Years ago, a business associate took Annie and me aside and chided us for what he called our "exclusivity." "You each need to develop a friend of the opposite sex," he said, "someone you could go to the movies with, or out to dinner alone with." Interestingly, though, later in the evening he confided that he'd had to legally adopt one of his own children since he discovered the child was actually fathered by his best friend. It sounded to us as if he needed "exclusivity" more than we needed "broadening"!

We've found that many Christian leaders we highly respect share our cautions, even if they do appear to be prudish. I read recently that Billy Graham has made it a practice through the years never to be alone with any woman except his wife in a car or restaurant. (A London newspaper thought they'd stumbled onto a scandal when they got word that Dr. Graham had dinner with someone named Beverly Shea. The scandal lost its sizzle, however, when they discovered the person involved was actually *George* Beverly Shea, the soloist for the crusade!)

When you value what you have, you do what it takes to protect it. And of course, preventative actions like this leave no room at all for dabbling with pornography or sexually provocative movies. We want to avoid everything that makes sex anything less than the wonderful gift of God it actually is, and to avoid anything that suggests to us someone besides each other would better meet our needs.

Keeping a sexual commitment involves more than just what we *don't* do. Following Christ isn't just adhering to a bunch of don'ts. Rather, it's a holy adventure focused on

---

[4]Jerry Jenkins, *Moody Monthly*, (July/August 1987), 6.

what we *do* with Him and for Him and through Him. And we believe this is just as true for faithfulness in marriage. Staying faithful doesn't involve just not sleeping with someone other than your spouse. It means putting your best effort and energy into enhancing the romance you have with your mate. In other words, faithfulness is more than just saying no to others; it's also saying yes to your spouse.

One of my favorite ways to keep on saying yes to this woman God has given me is to plan second honeymoons. This "custom" began with us during a particularly difficult time in our life together. I was still on the road and we never had the time together we needed. I loved Annie, but I wanted a way to show her. Thus was born the idea for a second honeymoon.

I secretly arranged for my mother to keep Nathan and Heidi for a weekend, and made a reservation at a motel out of town. Annie says now that weekend marked a turning point in our life together. When she saw the effort I took, she became convinced in a deeper way than she ever had before of my love for her.

That second honeymoon turned out to be the first of many, and through experience (and the experiences of other couples who've tried it, as well), we've come up with some suggestions for creating a second honeymoon of your own.

I suggest the husband take the initiative in planning the second honeymoon. Women usually seem to be quicker to understand the need for time alone together, so be prepared to pick your wife up off the floor after she faints when you announce what you've planned.

If you want the weekend to be a surprise (and that makes it more fun, of course), you'll need to sneakily find out if the date you've chosen is clear for her. You'll want to avoid her monthly period. And if you want to display an incredible amount of sacrifice, plan your second honeymoon on either Superbowl weekend, the start of the World Series, or during the NBA playoffs.

If you have children, you'll have need of a sitter. Never call a prospective sitter and say, "You wouldn't want to keep my kids for thirty-six hours, would you? I probably shouldn't have asked . . . oh, never mind!"

Instead, be honest, but positive, asking the sitter if she would take your kids so that you and your wife can have some much-needed time together.

The price you have to pay for a sitter will vary according to your time away and number of kids you have. But tell the sitter up front what you plan to pay to avoid any confusion. The sitter should know what reward he or she can expect for such bravery.

Most importantly, make sure the sitter is dependable. Neither you nor your wife want to be worrying about the kids while you're away. Leave the number of your place of lodging with the sitter, but also give strict instructions *not to call* unless she's being tied to a post and the kids are lighting matches.

I recommend staying in a motel for two reasons. A motel is usually more romantic, and also the two of you won't have to clean it when you leave as you would if you stayed, for example, in a friend's cabin. Choose a motel that's not more than one to three hours away. After all, who wants to spend the whole weekend driving? You might even want to go back to the same place you spent your first honeymoon, and even request the same room. When you make the reservation, ask to have your confirmation number mailed to you. Sometimes motel clerks are forgetful, and you don't want to arrive and find your room has someone else in it.

Call a florist in advance and arrange for flowers to be placed in your room. Be sure the message you add to the bouquet sets a romantic tone for your time together. And when you pack, include a nice, fragrant candle. (It'll not only sweeten the air in your room, but the candlelight does wonders for untanned, wrinkled and cellulite-dimpled bodies.)

When you arrive, ask the Lord to purify the room and fill it with His love.

While you're away, you'll spend at least *some* of the time talking. Don't talk about the kids. This time is meant to remind you that you are not only Mom and Dad, you are husband and wife, lovers and friends. Avoid, too, talking about business, or all that other daily-life junk that fills up space but doesn't draw you closer. You're alone with a woman you're out to attract, impress and enjoy. There'll be time to solve the problems with the plumber's bill and Johnny's math grades when you get home.

Make the entertainment fun for both of you. Don't plan to go to a ball game, unless she's a big fan. Generally, do nothing that will make her feel as if she's just tagging along on your hobby weekend. Try to avoid theaters, because you'll wind up spending three hours watching other people relate to each other, rather than getting closer yourselves. And especially avoid the television. If you wanted to spend your time with Bill Cosby or the Oakland A's, you should have saved your money, and stayed home.

Be full of surprises. Try writing her a poem and stashing it in her luggage when she's not looking. Or buy a card that expresses how you feel about her. Get her some of her favorite perfume, or bring along a cassette player with her favorite tapes.

Plan at least one nice meal in a romantic restaurant. (If you're like me, you'll need to pray for grace to refrain from asking the manager to turn up the lights so you can see what you're eating.) You might also want to take along some snacks, such as grapes, cheese and crackers etc. (If all goes well, you may find you never want to leave your room! You didn't on your first honeymoon, did you?)

I've assumed in these instructions that I'm talking to men. But I know, too, some women will wait a lifetime for their husbands to pull off a romantic get-away. If that's true for you, then you can certainly feel free to initiate a second honeymoon. Or you can plan it together. However it happens, be sure it comes off.

So much of marriage involves sharing the daily grind. We need to make room for the pleasure as well, either to regenerate the electricity between us, or to keep it arcing as it did at the start. We need to keep filling up each other's "cup of love."

> Something happens when a pretty young girl
> Smiles at a married man.
> It'll take him back for a moment;
> Then he'll wonder just where he stands.
> And if his cup of love is empty 'cause he can't
>   drink at home,
> When another woman offers her drink
> Temptation comes on strong.
>
> Now a woman can see when there's lust in the
>   eyes
> Of a man who is looking her way.
> And even though she's married there's something
>   exciting
> In the kind words a stranger might say.
> And if her cup of love is empty 'cause she can't
>   drink at home,
> When another man offers his drink
> Temptation comes on strong.
>
> You gotta keep his cup filled up with love

And don't ever let it run dry.
Keep her drinking at home and when she's out
    there alone
It'll help her let temptation go on by.[5]

Love Was Never Meant to Be Generic

ANNIE: Today, we've become infatuated with personalizing our lives. It started innocently enough—we engraved our initials on jewelry, or stitched them on sweaters, or etched them on crystal.

But from this humble beginning, a massive industry devoted to personalizing has grown. Stationery and key rings and mugs and T-shirts all come emblazoned with your name. Your home can be resplendent with welcome mats, mailboxes, table linens, and Christmas ornaments all bearing your insignia. Your kids can sport personalized schoolbags and swim-team jackets, and read storybooks with their own names printed into the text. Every other computer-generated advertising letter stuffed in your mailbox uses your name more times than your mother does when she writes you.

In the heat of this passion to personalize our world, we have overlooked the most important facet of our lives: We have failed to personalize the way we say "I love you."

Breaking Away From Generic Love

When we were first married, I heard a message from a lady in California who claimed to know all about wifing. If a woman loved her husband, this woman insisted, she'd fix him breakfast in bed. Until then, all our meals had been eaten in an upright position, but I was anxious to do well at loving my man, so breakfast in bed it would be.

Unfortunately, Steve did not respond well to this innovation. California husbands must have some inbred athletic prowess he lacks, because juggling that tiny little tray on his knees as he tried to keep from seeding the sheets with biscuit crumbs was too much to handle.

But I was determined to show I loved him. The next suggestion I came across in one of those "keeping-the-sizzle-in-your-marriage" books insisted on candlelight dinners as the key to bliss. So the lights went down, and the candles were ignited.

But Steve had a bad experience once with food he couldn't see, so he associated candlelight with nausea rather than passion. He's since gotten over this aversion, but at the time my idea was a flop. So once again I felt a failure.

After the candlelight fiasco, I came to a new conclusion. Perhaps these well-meaning teachers spoke so highly of these expressions of love because they'd married men who liked to eat in strange places. Maybe the secret to their success was not the bedside breakfasts, but rather that they'd studied their husbands long enough to know their likes and dislikes. What a new thought!

Spurred on by these conclusions, I started a study of Steve to find out how *he* liked to hear "I love you." Some of the answers I came up with proved to be unconventional, at best.

When Love Means Scratching the "Sock Ridges"

Steve was born with inordinately large calves. I assume that when God designed him, He planned them as an asset to a boy from West Virginia who'd spend untold hours trudging up and down those Appalachian hills. But having calves shaped like upside-down bowling pins has its drawbacks. For one thing, his socks slide down as fast as he can pull them up, so when he jogs, he's had to resort to wearing socks with a thick elastic band around the top. Though they don't sag, the elastic also carves grooves around his ankles that feel miserable.

When he comes in from a hard run, he claims there's no experience closer to heaven than getting those ridges in his ankles scratched. In my study of Steve, I took note of this quirk, and appointed myself Official Ankle-Ridge Itch Remover. When he strips off his sweat socks, I invite him to plunk his feet in my lap, and I scratch those ridges while he lies there on the floor with his tongue hanging out like a dog.

I'm willing to bet you've never read a marriage book that recommends ankle-scratching as a way to express your love to your mate—and you're not reading it now, either! This particular way to say "I love you" does wonders for our life together only because it's *tailored to us.*

Nongeneric Love Works for Men, Too

My creativity pushed Steve to take a look at his adeptness as a lover. Did he love me? Of course he did, and in the generic expressions of love he was doing great. He'd married me, hadn't he? And forsaken all others for me . . . and hustled to earn a living so he could provide for me. . . . Steve didn't beat me; he thanked me for cooking dinner and kissed me goodbye whenever he left the house.

But what I needed was to have that generic love *personalized*. I needed him to find my "ankle ridges," too. So Steve started a study of his own. One that he discovered came at the kids' bedtime. After a long day, I can be short on the energy it takes to oversee the baths, the teeth-brushing, the story-telling and tucking-in that two kids require. On those days, if he offers to take over pajama duty, his action shouts "I love you" more loudly than dozens of roses ever could.

Of course, your wife might insist on flowers as her most meaningful expression of your love. Or your husband may choose your companionship at a Cubs game over breakfast in bed. Sometimes personalized love does mean presents. Other times it means giving *your presence* in a special way.

How Do I Love Thee? Let Me Find the Ways

Have you seen books that offer 1,001 ways to love your spouse? If you've been tempted to buy one, the suggestion I'm about to offer will save you the trouble . . . and $10.95. You don't need 1,001 ways to love a spouse. More than likely, 945 of them won't mean much to your mate, anyway.

Just sit down with your partner and ask, "What would you like me to give you or do for you to let you know how much I love you?"

Getting answers to this question will not only enhance your life together, it can save you much pain—as the Wrights discovered.

Even though they'd just moved into a beautiful new home, there was no time to relax in front of the magnificent stone fireplace or enjoy lazy Saturdays by their pool because Tim was never home. Finally, his wife could take no more.

"I feel as if you don't love me because you're working all the time," she told him through her tears.

Tim looked bewildered. "I was working so much *because* I love you. I wanted you to have the house you've always talked about. But I can't afford the payments without all this extra overtime. I don't like being gone so much, but I did it because pleasing you matters to me."

Tim believed money equalled love because of what he'd seen in his parents' life. His mother could only see affection in high-priced gifts. Tim assumed his wife held the same values. His incorrect assumption needlessly turned an act of love into a source of contention.

How does your mate need to hear "I love you"? Have you asked? Have you studied your spouse to find the answers for yourself?

Steve's dad did. That's why I can remember his mother saying, "The carpet in this room has been easy to keep clean because Steve's father has always left his shoes on the porch when he comes home from the factory." He had the good sense to study his woman and find out what said love to her. I want to do the same. I want to become a Steve-ologist, so thoroughly in touch with this man I live with that he never lacks for love given in the form he wants it most.

Sometimes I'm motivated to this kind of giving from my great love for Steve. But other times I do it simply because I'm a reasonable woman. We Chapmans have promised to be together until death parts us, right? So since we have to journey together, why not be as happy as we can along the way?

I see it this way, from a female viewpoint. Most men provide adequately, work hard and don't beat their wives. But most, it seems, are also unromantic. When you plan a nice meal and light the candles, you can count on them to ask if the electricity has been turned off.

Many men have been taught from childhood that being

romantic means being sentimental and syrupy-sweet—in other words, anything but manly. Perhaps your man's aversion to romance was even appealing to you when you were dating. Maybe that coolheaded objectivity and *macho* image that he portrayed felt exciting to you then. But now you miss the romantic niceties, and you're not sure your *macho* man is capable of change.

So where does this leave you? It seems to me you have several choices, each with its own set of consequences.

You could spend the rest of your married life resenting the man God has given you, and become an expert at pity-party planning.

You can dedicate the remainder of your earthly days to becoming the world's greatest nag, thus making your husband miserable.

You could decide to suffer in silence, making yourself miserable. Or, you can submit your life to God's care and decide to dwell on your husband's good qualities. Then do all you can to create an atmosphere of love and warmth in your home.

I like that fourth option myself, and my husband does, too. We're stuck with each other now, so we've decided to make of it what we can. And you know, finding these special ways to please each other has made the trip a lot more fun.

Staying Tuned-in

Personalized love isn't static, so don't expect to sit down with your spouse one day to cement in place a lifetime list of ways you can best give your love. If you are doing things right in your marriage, each of you is going to change and grow. In his instructions in Ephesians 5, God tells husbands to nourish their wives.

When we nourish our tomatoes with plant food, they grow. When we nourish our kids with Wheaties, they get bigger. And when Steve provides emotional food to satisfy my "soul hunger," I grow, too. With growth comes change. As I grow, he needs to listen for the new ways I want to hear "I love you." The same holds true for husbands. As I respect and complete Steve, he grows. My expressions of love for him need to adjust to the man he's becoming.

One woman I know reflected on these changes as she talked about the computer her husband had given her for her birthday.

"When we first married, if he'd have given me an expensive machine I'd have been furious. I was terribly uncertain about my own womanliness, so a gift like this would have confirmed my worst fears. It would have labeled me businesslike and competent . . . in other words, a workhorse. I would have seen it as an appropriate gift for a business partner, but *not* something he'd have given Raquel Welch. So for those early birthdays he came through with perfume and outrageous, lacy things and other tangible evidences that assured me I was attractive to him.

"Now it's twelve years later, and I'm much more sure of my femininity. I've begun to dream some professional dreams I didn't have before. For instance, I'm taking steps to turn my interest in accounting into a legitimate business. My husband let me know he sees and supports how I've changed by investing a sizable chunk of money in a data processing setup for me. When I protested about the cost, he waved me off. 'You can't do your work without the right tools,' he said. Do you see why I continue to be so crazy about this man?"

If Your Partner Doesn't Return Personalized Love

What a pleasure when you've worked hard to see love as your mate does, and he or she returns the favor. When both of you give—and *get*—you find marital oneness at its best.

But what about when the giving is one-sided? What then?

You can teach your mate the ways you'd like to receive love. Just as some people take more naturally to ice skating or song writing or cooking than others do, some of us have built-in relational capacities others lack. In marriage, it's common to find couples in which a *relater* pairs with a *non-relater.* Your spouse may suffer from dulled nerve endings when it comes to picking up your vibrations. Maybe your spouse doesn't personalize love because he or she just plain can't figure out what you need.

You may need to be the teacher, listening to yourself to find out which love expressions mean most and then passing on your observations to your partner. Don't be discouraged, however, if it takes more than one ten-minute talk to communicate what you mean.

From the beginning of our marriage I've always been very verbal. If I felt Steve hadn't been giving me enough attention, I'd say, "Steve, I need more attention."

I made the directions simple and straightforward.

"Steve, I need you to tell me you love me."

Or, "Tell me I'm pretty."

Or, "Tell me I'm your best friend."

After he'd accommodate me, I'd thank him and go on with my business.

You may not think a compliment is worth much if you have to ask for it. In times past, I would have agreed with you. But finally it occurred to me that my husband could not read my mind. If he was going to meet my needs, he'd have to know what those needs were. The book of Proverbs teaches that "a man dies from lack of instruction." I believe a relationship can die while you wait for your partner to learn to read your mind and understand your needs.

Some husbands and wives are easier to teach than others. One woman we know realized she needed her husband's love to come in the form of what she called "affection when the lights are on." She wanted him to hold her hand as they walked together, or put his arm around her as they watched television, or catch her eye at a church supper in one of those "you're-mine-and-I'm-glad" kind of glances they gave each other during their courtship. "He's tender and affectionate when the lights are out," she said, "but when the daylight comes, he freezes."

This woman isn't unique in her desire. F. B. Dresslar reports that a woman, in particular, needs eight to ten meaningful touches each day just to maintain physical and emotional health. And more than eighty percent of a woman's desire for meaningful touch is nonsexual.[1]

Though she mentioned these desires to her husband several times, he'd always mumble something about "not being a very touchy person." And nothing changed.

Then, during one particularly intimate moment, she approached the topic again. But this time she took a tack he could understand. "I explained to him that not having this daytime affection was as devastating to me as it would be for him if we gave up making love. *That he could grasp!* And though he'll never need all the hugs and squeezes I do, he's now working harder to become more 'touchy,' as he calls it. It just took time and the right moment to help him understand what I was saying."

You can also appreciate the love your partner does have to give. Some husbands or wives feel unnecessarily unloved. Their mate does, in fact, love them and show it, but they refuse to read the love signs as they are posted.

---

[1]Gary Smalley and John Trent, *The Language of Love* (Pomona, Calif.: Focus on the Family Publishing, 1988), 123.

A woman may wish her husband would "say it with flowers," and indeed, he should, since that's how she wants to hear love. But to accuse him of a lack of love may be unfair. Perhaps he's broadcasting costly love when he spends a Saturday wallpapering the family room because she wants to change the color scheme. He'd rather be golfing, but for love, he chooses paste over a putter. We need to challenge ourselves to personalize our love, but at the same time, let's not reject the pleasure of the love we're offered, even if it isn't packaged exactly right.

You can give personalized love anyway. Your mate may need long-term exposure to an example of personalized love before he or she gets the idea. After all, Jesus took this approach with us. Perhaps your story is like mine. Christ wooed me for years before I responded to Him. How glad I am He didn't give up when I didn't respond quickly. Because He patiently and persistently gives himself to us, you and I can give to our mate without a ready return.

So go ahead. Pass your spouse the generic raisin bran or offer a cup of generic coffee. But when it comes to loving, don't settle for generics. Make your caring personally tailored to the one you love.

Snuggles

One day, in the afternoon, I saw my lady sad
I said, "What have I done to make you feel so
    bad?"
She said, "Nothing."
I said, "That's not true.
Now tell me what have I done to you."
She said, "It's nothing you've done.
It's something you didn't do."

She said, "I need your snuggles.

The day's a struggle without them.
When we miss those times, I seem to feel alone.
When I can remember you, warm on a chilly
     morning,
It helps me think of you through the day.
And when you're on my mind, everything's
     okay."

Sometimes, in the morning now,
I remember that afternoon,
And how I learned of my lady's needs
And now I don't leave so soon.
It's getting easy for me to stay
And give her some time of my day,
'Cause when I wake up,
I can still hear her sayin',

"I need your snuggles,
The day's a struggle without them.
When we miss those times, I seem to feel alone.
When I can remember you, warm on a chilly
     morning,
It helps me think of you through the day.
And when you're on my mind, everything's
     okay."[2]

When the Going Gets Tough, the Tough Stay Right Where They Are

STEVE: If there's nothing in your life you'd be willing to die for, then you don't have anything to live for, either.

What I'm talking about is commitment. It's what Jesus talked about when He told the story of a man who found a valuable pearl in a field. The man went at once and sold everything he had to buy the field so the pearl could be his. If the pearl later turned out to be worthless, he'd be left with nothing, because he'd risked all he had to own it.

Commitment. It's what the Spanish explorer Cortes insisted on when he landed in Mexico. When he saw his crew's fear and vacillation about invading this land of the Aztecs, Cortes gathered them all on shore and then set fire to the vessels on which they'd come. Now there could be no turning back; they were committed.

Commitment is a man and woman, standing together before God and His people, pledging to forsake all others and cleave only to each other, until death—and only death—parts them.

135

Or at least that's what marriage was meant to be.

God created it to show a watching world the loving, exclusive, permanent union of Jesus Christ and His people.

But our generation has decided to remake marriage to suit our convenience. We decided this "exclusive" stuff was too much trouble, so we promoted "open marriage." When you understand the deep and eternal bonding that happens between two people when they marry, you laugh at how ridiculous it is to try to combine "open" and "marriage" together in one phrase. It makes about as much sense as trying to talk about a humble politician, or jumbo shrimp. Marriage cannot be open and still be marriage. After all, that's why they call it "wed*lock*," isn't it?

And instead of a permanent union, we decided it should have to hold out "only as long as our love [i.e., these gushy feelings] shall last." Sticking together without a tidal wave of feelings to carry you has become unthinkable.

Tim Stafford, who for the last thirteen years has written in *Campus Life* magazine on love and sex, talks about the flaws in our insistence that we all deserve "compatible" partners.

Stafford says that in contemporary thinking,

> Compatibility just happens—you "click." Of course, people do change over time, so couples who are compatible today may not "click" tomorrow. [To us], happy, lifelong monogamy is less a triumph of the will than a miracle of compatibility. You hope you and your lover can stay balanced on the bubble [of intimacy] indefinitely. But you admit the forces of fate may ruin your plans.[1]

---

[1]Tim Stafford, "Intimacy, Our Latest Sexual Fantasy," *Christianity Today* (January 16, 1987), 23.

One Christian man showed his belief in the "compatibility myth" when he said,

> I married her at eighteen, and right then we seemed like a great fit. In the years after, we both changed so much we no longer made each other happy. Surely no one expects me to have to be chained for a lifetime to the immature choice I made as a teenager.

Of course you can't, not if you believe marriage is like signing up for the Book-of-the-Month Club. As long as it leaves you stimulated and happy and fulfilled, you keep up your membership. But when it no longer provides these benefits, you're free to drop out and connect with someone else who *currently* seems to promise these benefits.

Counteracting this belief, Stafford goes on to explain:

> Nowhere does the Bible say that love is the basis for marriage; marriage is the basis for love. Paul's command is "Husbands, love your wives" rather than "Men, marry your lovers." Marriage is a covenant that's to be filled with love, as a cup is filled with wine. But of the two, the cup is necessary before the wine is poured.

It's been our purpose in these pages to help you learn to keep your mate's cup filled up with love. But if the days come when he or she isn't filling your cup, those will be the moments to go back to the commitment you made, and ask God to help you keep it.

It may be for your children's sake that you stay true to your marriage commitment. Divorce has become such an easy part of the vocabulary for most of us that we gloss over the vast devastation it wreaks on a child when parents divorce.

Studies and statistics on the children of divorce are one

thing. It's another to have these children on your block, and see the pain of their wounds in their eyes. Not long ago, we took a couple of the neighborhood kids, whose parents were divorcing, with us to the gym for the evening. On the way, these kids described to ours what it was like to be living in a home where everything they counted on was falling down around them. The little girl told of her mother's crying and screaming; of her daddy who closed his ears to it all; of seeing everything she owned thrown into cardboard boxes to be taken off to a strange apartment.

My heart broke for these two helpless victims of the cruelest of wars, a war in which there are no heroes and no winners—just wounded, hurting casualties on every side.

Besides your children, there's another, even more powerful reason, to keep on with your marriage commitment, even through the toughest of times. God hates divorce. (And if you've been through this havoc, or are close to someone who has, you understand why.) So your desire to honor and obey Him can pull you on toward choosing to keep your marriage vows, even if your partner hasn't.

I know that some of you reading these words *did* keep on through the toughest of times, but your home broke up anyway. You loathe divorce, yet now you find yourself alone. One Christian woman whose husband abandoned her for another said, "I wake up every morning thinking, 'This *cannot* be happening to me!' But it was, and she had to call on all the grace and strength and courage her faith could muster to pick up the broken pieces and build a new life for herself and her children.

Some of you who have been through this living hell could write much more powerfully than I about the importance of keeping a marriage commitment. You know from personal experience the devastation that comes when a home falls apart. And I commend you to the loving care of your faithful heavenly Father, the only One with power enough to bring beauty from ashes and joy from mourning.

But if you are married, fight for your marriage with all that's within you. Exhaust every available opportunity to make the marriage work. I talked to a couple who had been married thirty-nine years. They'd been through some stormy times, but in their tenth year of marriage came the bout to end all bouts. The wife got so mad she pulled her suitcase out of the bedroom closet and started packing.

"What are you doing?" her husband demanded.

"I'm leaving."

So without a word he got his suitcase and started filling it with his clothes.

"Now, what are *you* doing?" his wife asked, bewildered.

"If you're leaving," he told her firmly, "I'm going with you."

There was a man determined to do what it took to keep his marriage together. And determination is sometimes what it takes. You may be feeling right now that you've lost the determination or the will to fight. Be sure of this. If you choose on behalf of your family, God will respond to you. Your commitment to Him will move Him to commit himself to you and to marshall the power and grace of heaven on your behalf and on behalf of your family. When you choose to follow Christ, even though the price to you seems overwhelming, Christ commits himself to be with you. "He who honors me, him will my Father honor" (John 12:26).

And from time to time, we need to put our commitment into words. I don't believe I've ever given my wife or children cause to wonder whether or not I'm going to give the rest of my life to them. But after that heart-wrenching episode in the car with our neighbor's children, Nathan said to me, "Daddy, is this going to happen to us? Are you going to leave us?"

If I hadn't been driving the car, I'd have taken that little boy in my arms. But instead I told him firmly, "Son, I am committed to your mother, to you and to Heidi. I promised God a long time ago that I would stay in this family, and I will."

Nathan said nothing for a moment, but it seemed that even this clear affirmation wasn't yet enough.

"Promise?"

"Yes, Son, I promise."

Whew! Seeing how much my family needed this kind of confirmation has prompted me several times since to look for chances to make my commitment clear to them. More than once I've gathered the children near us and said, "Annie, I love you and I am going to stay with you regardless of what may happen." Then I turn to each of the children and re-state my intentions to them. And Annie commits herself to each of us as well. Then we end with a prayer of thanks to God for His faithfulness and tell Him, too, that we promise to be faithful to *Him.*

Two other things help strengthen me to stand by my commitment. One is the encouragement of other believers who understand the importance of marriage and whose example gives me courage when I need it in sticking through the good times and the bad. People like my parents, who've just finished over forty years of serving Christ and each other. People like James Dobson and our friends at Focus on the Family, who've not only held high God's desires for marriage, but have taught us how to make those desires reality. And some of our wonderful friends who insist that we be nothing but the best for Jesus' sake.

The other real resource of strength has been learning to pray with Annie. Praying *for* her is one thing; praying *with* her quite another. It was a grace I've needed to learn, but it's been well worth the effort.

One of the first times Annie and I tried this business of praying together happened back when we were dating. We were driving along in Sarah, that old '50 Chevy I told you about before, on the way to church one night in the rain, when Sarah died. Or sort of died. She didn't lose her engine power, but she couldn't go forward anymore.

I was steaming. "I'm gonna have to get out and walk in this rain. And that gas station is probably a mile back or more," I sputtered between clenched teeth.

But Annie held out her hand to me and said sweetly, "Let's pray for Sarah."

When she made the suggestion, I got even madder . . . mostly because she'd suggested it and it wounded my ego. (If she'd just given me another forty-five minutes or so, I'm sure I would have come up with the idea.)

I may have an ego, but I'm no fool. I realized right away I had two options. I'd either have to pray with Annie or get out and start walking in that rain. So I took her hand.

To be honest, I had never prayed for a car before. (Up to this time I'd never had to, because I'd always driven Fords!) Even though my faith was weak, I bowed my head and prayed, "Oh, Master Mechanic, Sarah's sick. We don't know what's wrong with her, Lord, and we have to come to you because we don't know whom else to go to. And we're on our way to church. Please heal Sarah. Lord, I never prayed for a car before, but I believe all things are possible with you. Amen."

Well, I put the key back in old Sarah and started up the engine. It started fine, but that wasn't the problem. The real test was still ahead. I pushed in the clutch, dropped her down into first, started giving her a little bit of gas. When I let out on the clutch, I mean to tell you . . . I never felt a tighter chassis. That transmission took hold and we hit the highway so smoothly I didn't even have time to look back.

I was driving down the road yelling, *"Wow!*—a brand new car! Lord, while you're at it, could you heal the play in this steering wheel?" My faith was so exuberant that if there'd been a dead man lying along the road, I probably would have stopped and yelled, "You, get up!"

All right, I got a little carried away. But some of us need more dramatic experiences than others to get us started. In the years since, we've not consistently gotten such instantaneous and exciting results. We've had times when we've been praying in one direction and God is going in another. But the times Annie and I have spent in prayer have done more than anything else to bind us together in a love that's bigger than our own. Talking to God has refueled us to serve each other out of love for Christ, and because of that service our romance continues to grow. We believe it, because God's Word says so and because we're seeing it work in our life together.

Even with these resources, though, I sometimes feel as if our marriage is a tiny outpost in the midst of enemy territory and enemy troops are shooting at us from every side.

Time pressure. The push to do it all and meet everyone's expectations. *Ka-boom!*

Temptations to indulge in immoral thoughts or relationships, or to choose money or success over God's plan for us. *Blam!*

Trials from the wear-and-tear of life and the pain of those around us whose suffering touches us so deeply. *Pow!*

Somehow in the midst of this onslaught, these moments of recommitment strengthen and refocus me. I may do many things with my life, but if I fail my family nothing else matters as much. They are the pearl of great price, fully worth giving all I own.

In their powerful book *The Language of Love*, Gary Smalley and John Trent have an important message for those of us who are trying to live out God's plan for marriage in the face of all kinds of opposition. I'll let them tell in their own words the story of a man who found hope in a hopeless situation. The man you'll meet is a young Marine, the time is World War II and the place is the island of Iwo Jima.

––––––––––––

The date was February 21, 1945—two days after the landing. Jerry had taken cover in a small crater formed by an exploding artillery shell. The shelling from back in the mountains had kept everyone awake almost all night. The morning had dawned with falling rain and restless fog drifting in the distant, higher slopes. But when the skies cleared and the Japanese could pick out their targets, the artillery bursts were joined by small-arms fire.

Jerry had already given up all hope of coming off the island alive. Of the fourteen men in his rifle section, only he and five others hadn't been wounded or killed. In just two days, he had already seen far too much death. But its cruel hand was just beginning to strike: More Marines would die on Iwo Jima than on all the other battlefields of World War II combined. So many had died or been wounded around him already that he felt he had as much chance of living as keeping a soap bubble from bursting in the wind.

That's when his corporal crawled up next to him and flashed him a grin. "You still alive, Jerry?" he said in his southern accent, offering Jerry a swig from a priceless canteen of water. "We're gaining on them, you know."

"How do you know that?" Jerry answered back with

a thin smile. "Nobody came running up to me with a white flag last night."

"Look here, son, I have it on good authority. Tomorrow you'll see our boys on top of that hill. We're going to make it." Then he looked up at the fog-tipped volcano and spoke the words Jerry has never forgotten: "You'll see the flag tomorrow."

From the time the Marines first sighted Iwo Jima from the decks of their ships, they had been looking up at the highest point on the island. It was the top of Mount Suribachi, an extinct volcano. It was only 550 feet high, but the way death rained down from its steep, ragged slopes, it seemed more like Mount Everest. To have the American flag up there would mean that—at least from this hill— death would have lost its frightening foothold. It would also be the best sight any Marine had seen since he had landed.

As events turned out, Jerry wouldn't see the flag for another two days. And his corporal would never see it. He was killed in action that night. But on February 23, 1945, the hill was taken.

As the Stars and Stripes flew above them for the first time, men all over the island stood and cheered, ignoring the risk of exposing their positions.

When Jerry saw the flag, the words his corporal had spoken came back in full force. And those same words would give him strength to carry on during the next eight days until he was critically wounded and carried off the island.

"When I got off Iwo alive, I felt my life had been given back to me," Jerry said. "You never forget something like that. In the years since, whenever I've had things go wrong I remember my corporal's words. When things look their toughest, I just think back and say to myself, 'Hang in there, Jerry. You'll see the flag tomorrow.' "[2]

If you're hanging on in the midst of a tough marriage, then let me encourage you that God will not forget you. You, too, will see the flag tomorrow. You can say with Solomon, "His banner over me is love!" (Song of Sol. 2:4).

Someone asked the French general Napoleon to explain his defeat at Waterloo. The British didn't win, he said, because they had a better trained army or because they were better equipped. They weren't victorious because they had more soldiers. The British took the battle, Napoleon believed, because they fought five minutes longer.

Sometimes I wonder what battles we've lost because we stop fighting five minutes before the Lord is ready to raise the flag of victory. We so badly need to hold on to Him and to the commitments we've made.

God will grace us with what we need to honor Him.

It's impossible for me to think of God's provision of grace without Linda and Mike coming to mind. This beautiful couple had it all. Linda was a former Miss Texas beauty pageant contestant, a concert pianist and a deeply committed Christian. Mike loved Christ, too. And because he came up in the oil business during the boom years, his career took off like a gusher. They had it all.

But Linda caught a virus, which inexplicably moved into the lining of her brain. Within days this vibrant young woman lay comatose in a hospital bed awaiting death.

By God's grace Linda survived, though doctors predicted she'd never be much more than a vegetable. But she fought her way back and can now walk, though with

---

[2]Gary Smalley and John Trent, *The Language of Love* (Pomona, Calif.; Focus on the Family Publishing, 1988), 87–89.

a stiff-legged and unsteady gait. She can talk, too, though her speech is slow and labored.

But as great as the miracle of her recovery is the miracle of the love God has given Mike for his wife. Just two weeks before Linda's illness struck, the Lord burdened Mike with a desire to grow deeper in his love for his wife. "Lord," he prayed, "let me love my wife as Christ loved the Church." I believe that, with that prayer, God was graciously preparing Mike for what was to come. In less than fourteen days, Mike would know what it meant to give himself in love to someone who had nothing at all to give back. How much more clearly could we picture the kind of love Christ has for us?

In the months after, Mike needed to provide for Linda's every need, and was given little hope of seeing progress. Another man might have left—or stayed, but with resentment and self-pity. Instead, Mike radiates love for Linda, not the Hollywood kind of meaningless mush that turns tail at the first hint of adversity. He shows a strong, giving love, the kind of love that could cause Jesus to face the horror of the cross and count it all joy.

Seeing their love is why—

We believe a man and wife
Would have a better married life
If they would try out-serving one another.

For deeper love is felt
When what is done is not for self
But when it's done to satisfy the other.

We pray God's blessings on you as you fan the home fires through your service to each other and to Christ.

Home Fires

Oh, my lovely lady, on the day I married you,
I felt the flames of love so real

When I said, "I do." And sometimes it may seem
Like those flames are burnin' low,
But, darlin', I still love you and I want you to
    know

I'm gonna keep the home fires burnin',
I'll keep the home fires burnin',
I want to keep the home fires burnin'
Just for you.

Listen to me, children,
This is from your Father's heart,
I know there'll be sometimes
When you and I are far apart.
And when you're out there in the world
It may get dark and cold.
You'll need a place to go
Where it's bright and warm
And I want you to know

I'm gonna keep the home fires burnin',
I'll keep the home fires burnin',
I want to keep the home fires burnin'
Just for you.[3]

Growing

11

ANNIE: Steve and I have never had much success with sharing a regular Bible-reading and prayer time. As we've told you, we each read God's Word independently, but reading it together never became a habit. After our kids began to grow up, though, we felt a need to establish a regular time when our family met together for devotions.

Our children were less than enthusiastic. They could spend a whole evening watching *Little House on the Prairie* reruns with such intensity you'd think they were getting paid for it by the hour. But just let us mention it was time to read Scripture and it was as though they'd both been instantly struck with a terminal case of sleeping sickness. Their yawning and stretching and complaining and groaning could have easily put them in the running for an Emmy nomination.

But Steve grew up in a home where a "family altar" was as much a part of the daily routine as breakfast, so he especially was convinced we needed to get one going for ourselves. He and I decided we'd take a crack at reading enough verses each day to get through the Bible in a year.

As the year progressed, we did fairly well in fulfilling our goal. The only times that really discouraged us came when travel or concerts would cause us to miss a few days, and we'd have to play "catch up." What should have normally been a ten-to-fifteen minute session would stretch to forty-five minutes or an hour of Bible reading.

And being the conscientious Christian that he is, Steve was never content to just drone out the words. He was determined we'd know the deep truths of each passage. So, to assure we weren't letting our minds wander as he trudged us through some wilderness wandering in Numbers, he'd pick a bleary-eyed moment and hit us with a pop quiz on what he'd just read.

"Where did the children of Israel camp after they left Oboth?" he'd ask smugly. If we failed to dredge up the correct answer, he'd threaten to start all over! The children and I lived in mortal fear that Steve would catch the glazed look in our eyes, or glance up just as one of us let go a stifled yawn, and then the guilty party would be targeted for The Question. (As we went along, Steve and I began to take turns reading. When it was my night, you can guess who consistently wound up on the hot seat, trying to recall Bible information a theology professor wouldn't have known!)

Well, calendar pages turned, and so did the chapters of our Bible, and by Christmas we found ourselves with the end in sight. That's why on Christmas Day, Steve was determined we'd get our reading done *before* the gift explosion. My sister and her two-year-old, Billy, were visiting us, so before Steve began reading I turned on the video cam that was set up in the living room so we'd be able to treasure the memory of the beautiful tapestry of a loving family gathered to read Scripture before we shared our deep love through the giving of gifts.

Just before I turned on the camera, a thought occurred to me. "Steve," I sweetly inquired, "since it's Christmas, why don't we read the Christmas story instead of the assigned reading?" I didn't see this request as unreasonable, since by then we were stuck somewhere deep in the minor prophets.

"That would be fine," he answered, "but if we do, then we'll get behind and have to play 'catch up.' "

Those words struck terror in all our hearts, so reluctantly we agreed to stick to the schedule.

Billy, however, decided majority did not rule. Before him sat a Mount Everest of presents and he was ready to scale the heights. When his mother tried to explain about the great encouragement we were about to receive from the reading of God's Word, Billy let loose a barrage of protest only a two-year-old could create. It didn't take long to realize he had no intention of quitting, either, so Steve plowed ahead into the Scripture. It worked out all right, however, since the prescribed passage turned out to be one of those dreadful warnings with the children being brutally slaughtered and their bodies dashed to pieces. Blood was running down the streets and women were having their guts reamed out with swords. With a scriptural scenario like that, Billy's thrashing and moaning seemed somehow right in place.

By the time we hit the final verse, my sister was slumped on the sofa, sweaty and exhausted from trying to control her little tiger. Billy had moved into uttering those low guttural gasps that hang on when a child has exhausted himself with uncontrolled crying. My stomach was feeling as though dinner wasn't such a good idea after all, and our children were tensed like runners at the starting block, waiting for an okay to go for the gifts.

The best part of the evening came, though, when we realized we'd captured this mayhem on video tape, sound and all. (I have yet to get up the nerve to watch this film of the Chapmans Christmas Devotional Hour. You can bet the Billy Graham Association will never ask to make it into a family special.)

Well, we did persevere, and on December 31, we Chapmans held a major family celebration—we'd read through the entire Bible together. More importantly, we had an entire year of family devotions and all survived. We even found we'd grown from it.

When we started up again on January 1, we did decide to change the format a bit. We now read from an easier translation of the Bible and concentrate more on the New Testament. And we've added a time of prayer together.

You may have the idea our year of discipline produced perfect family devotions, but it didn't. During one recent moment of spiritual insanity, Steve and I decided it'd be more reverent if we gathered in a circle and got down on our knees to pray, bowing lowly before the Lord. But to our horror, the most unsavory thing started happening. The children—oh, how do I put this without being offensive? Well, let me simply say, I thought perhaps I needed to start fixing different foods for dinner. We let them know how irritated we were that they weren't exercising more control out of reverence for the Lord.

But God was on the kids' side. He quickly chided Steve and me that we were putting pressure on our children that He never intended. And if we were going to apply pressure, we'd have to live with the side effects as well. (We've since gone back to sitting on the couch for our prayer time, and it is working much better.)

If we've learned anything from these ventures into communal spiritual growth, it's the value of sticking with it, no matter what the odds. The benefits don't stop with the children, either. Steve and I often find we're more encouraged or instructed from our time than the children are.

We're wondering, too, if we would have had an easier time getting started with the kids if we'd established a regular devotional time together before our children were born.

Different couples find different ways for sharing spiritual growth.

Charlie and Martha Shedd have helped thousands of couples through their marriage books such as *Letters to Karen* and *Letters to Philip*. Like the rest of us, they had to work out their own method for devotions. They talked about their struggle in an interview with the editors of *The Wittenburg Door*, and their story is best told in their own words:

Charlie: [At the start of our marriage] we were becoming estranged from each other and we didn't want this estrangement. We decided to do something about it. We committed ourselves to (a) time with each other, (b) total honesty, (c) prayer. That's what we're really pushing for marriage: prayer! If we can get a couple to commit themselves for a duet of prayer, they can build a good marriage. Once they begin relating to the Lord, their relationship grows in depth.

If the two of you can't seem to pray together out loud, try what we did. We began our prayers in silence.

Martha: We have a favorite place where we sit down— a rocking loveseat in our living room. We hold hands and talk over the things we want to pray about. Anything that is troubling us, or something we're grateful for. Then we pray silently. We started this way and we still do it. Anybody can do that. Then we say the Lord's Prayer or "Amen" when we think we've gotten through.

Charlie: We have four goals at our house for a praying home.

Martha: One goal is that each of us has a quiet time every day. Charlie and I get up early and we have our quiet time . . . reading the Bible or inspirational books. This is our time of meditation. Another goal in our family is that everybody prays for everybody else every day. (There are thirteen now, including in-laws and grandchildren.) Third, we pray together as husband and wife. And our final goal is family devotions. We try to do that every day and we succeed most of the time, maybe seventy-five percent. It's a real celebration time.

Charlie: Back to the quiet time: Study is a big part of our prayer life. We study material together that we share with each other. Once in a while we read a book together. Martha reads to me or I read to her. We do this sometimes when we're in the car. But more often we read alone in our quiet time. We read the Bible. Then we discuss what we read. "I came on this verse, honey, and it said this to me. What do you think?"

Martha: We think discipline is all-important, but our prayer life isn't rigid. It's a relaxed discipline. And it's something we have a good time at—like our family devotions.[1]

———

The Shedds made a devotional time work because they found ways to adapt it. But sometimes we're reluctant to explore and experiment because of the guilt we feel. If I'm describing you, you'll be encouraged by Randy and Phyllis Michael's journey to find a meaningful way to share their spiritual life.

Phyllis said, "Another week had gone by and we still

---

[1] Philip Yancey, *After the Wedding* (Waco, Texas: Word Books, 1976), 147–148.

had not had 'family devotions.' I felt guilty and condemned. How could God be pleased with us—a pastor and his wife unable to find time [for] reading together, and praying. Interruptions or unexpected schedule changes often short-circuited our well-laid plans. The result: guilt feelings. Those little signs 'Ours Is a Family Altar Home' only added to my frustration. I had visions of everyone else happily gathered in loving, warm, family groups every day and having family devotions, while Randy and I remained spasmodic in our attempts."

Then one day Phyllis heard a Christian friend she admired confessing to struggles with family devotions. Phyllis suddenly felt less alone and more free to ask the Lord for a plan that might work in her life with Randy.

They decided to start right where they were. Since both already had a private time of Bible reading, they worked on making this more meaningful. Each continued to read a short passage daily, but began to answer questions about the passage according to a plan they call the "SMU Approach." "What does it *say*?" "What does it *mean*?" "How can I *use* it?"

Then they planned three or four times a week when they'd share with each other what they were learning from reading Scripture.

"For us it's been helpful to plan the week ahead on Sunday afternoon," Phyllis explained. "We mark on our calendars specific times for spiritual sharing, knowing that our plan is flexible. After each of us shares our discoveries from a particular passage, we then talk together about the implications of the verses for us. Often we will pray together about what we have found in the Word as it relates to our needs. Finally, we make some commitment to action on the basis of the Word.

"Many times we experience a closeness during our sharing that spreads into other areas of our relationship.

Our spirits commune and we experience a sense of our potential as a Christian couple."[2]

There's another side to shared spiritual growth that we value. Just as we're committed to support and encourage each other, we believe we're accountable to hold each other to high standards. Sometimes that's easy; other times it isn't.

Like the time when we were first married and went out for a burger. I wanted onion rings, but instead of stating my request I slid over in the booth, snuggled up next to Steve and in a little baby coo just dripping with come-on, I said, "Honey, could I have some onion rings?" No man with an ounce of hormones in his veins could have resisted!

But Steve turned straight toward me and firmly replied, "No."

No? Had I heard my new groom correctly?

"Annie," he said, "you were trying to manipulate me to get your way and that's not the right way for us to begin our life together."

I didn't speak to him for two days. But he was right. And how glad I've been in the years since that he expected me to act like the woman of God I want to be, even if holding me to God's standard cost him.

And he's been faithful more than once. I remember the time we drove from Nashville to Chicago to fulfill a singing engagement. We'd been told to prepare a forty-five-minute presentation, but after we arrived, we found out the organizers hadn't organized, and we wound up with five minutes instead. We'd driven six hours to sing two songs! I was steaming.

It turned out we came away with another chance to sing that night, but by concert time I was still furious. And

[2]*Happiness Is Growing a Marriage*, ed. Gene Van Note (Kansas City: Beacon Hill Press), 107–108.

my beloved decided I was in no spiritual condition to minister to anyone. Therefore I could not sing with him! While he did the concert, I was banished to the van like a naughty schoolgirl sent off to the corner.

Once again, he had to endure some moaning from me, but it reminded me that I trust him because he believes I belong to God first and to him second. And he expects me to hold him accountable as well.

I had to take my turn the night we sang for a special gathering of the program directors from a number of radio stations. Having these people like us could make a big difference in our career, and we wanted to succeed like never before. Our passion to make a good impression left us both so nervous we could barely sing. Steve had such a case of cotton-mouth he felt as if someone had stuffed a T-shirt down his throat. And to make things worse, during our performance, we began to hear snickers and laughing in the audience. With a bright spotlight shining right in our eyes, we couldn't even see the people in the first row, so we had no way of knowing the laughter was actually coming from a party next door and we assumed the audience was ridiculing our performance.

We left that stage as low as we'd ever been. We slunk off to the farthest booth in the darkest corner of a restaurant to hide out and lick our wounds. Steve was heading into the third chorus of "Poor Us" when it hit me. We were displeasing the Lord, and I stopped my husband in mid-whine.

"Honey," I told him, "the Lord may have shown us great mercy by letting us fail so miserably. We wanted to impress those people and make a name for ourselves. If we'd accomplished that we may have been on our way to becoming public successes, but failures in the eyes of God."

Steve didn't shower me with gratitude for these words

of admonition. What he wanted at that moment was a Pity Partner. But he did thank me later. And I knew I had freedom to share the correction because I know Steve wants to be God's man more than he wants to be coddled.

Helping each other grow in Christ can mean sharing times of correction as well as times in God's Word. But both are precious moments as deeper unity with Christ draws us more closely into each other than we've ever hoped to be.

Precious Moments

Our days have been filled with times to
    remember;
We've had moments with tears, and moments
    with laughter.
But the time has not ended, in this day God has
    loaned us.
What will we do, with these few precious
    moments?

I'll call the children, and I'll get the Letter
Before we're lost in our sleep, we'll gather
    together
And read from the heart of the God who has
    saved us
And kneel for a while, in His presence.

And these will be precious moments in His
    presence.
It's the best time we'll ever spend.
Our family's devoted to these precious moments
With Him.

Well, the children are busy; there are things I
    must do.
It seems so hard to carry it through

But it's always this way, it's always a fight
But let's not be defeated tonight.

For these will be precious moments in His
   presence.
It's the best time we'll ever spend.
Our family's devoted to these precious moments
With Him.[3]